God's Mighty Acts in
CREATION

God's Mighty Acts in
CREATION

Starr Meade

CROSSWAY

WHEATON, ILLINOIS

God's Mighty Acts in Creation
Copyright © 2010 by Educational Publishing Concepts, Inc.
Published by Crossway
         1300 Crescent Street
         Wheaton, Illinois 60187

Typesetting: Educational Publishing Concepts
Cover design: Amy Bristow
Cover illustrations: iStockphoto
First printing 2010
Printed in the United States of America

Unless otherwise indicated, Scripture quotations are from the ESV® Bible (*The Holy Bible, English Standard Version®*), copyright © 2001 by Crossway. Used by permission. All rights reserved.

Trade Paperback ISBN: 978-1-4335-1398-5
PDF ISBN: 978-1-4335-1399-2
Mobipocket ISBN: 978-1-4335-1400-5
ePub ISBN: 978-1-4335-2431-8

Library of Congress Cataloging-in-Publication Data
Meade, Starr, 1956–
  God's mighty acts in creation / Starr Meade.
    p. cm.
  ISBN 978-1-4335-1398-5 (tpb)—ISBN 978-1-4335-1399-2 (pdf)—ISBN 978-1-4335-1400-5
(mobipocket)—ISBN 978-1-4335-2431-8 (ePub)
  1. Creation—Juvenile literature. I. Title.

BS651.M399 2010
231.7'65—dc22   2010009997

Crossway is a publishing ministry of Good News Publishers.

VP   20 19 18 17 16 15 14 16 12 11 10
      11 10 9 8 7 6 5 4 3 2 1

For Katie, who sees and takes off her shoes

Contents

Creator and Creation: An Introduction

Day 1: Light and Water

Day 3: Land and Plants

Day 4: Sun, Moon, and Stars

Day 5: Birds and Fish

Day 6: Animals and People

Creator and Creation

An Introduction

What We Can See in Nature
Romans 1 and General Revelation

"For his invisible attributes, namely, his eternal power and divine nature, have been clearly perceived, ever since the creation of the world, in the things that have been made. So they are without excuse."

Romans 1:20

Are you a nature lover? You may not think of yourself as a nature lover, but I'm sure you are. The word the Bible uses for nature is "creation." You yourself are a creature, a part of creation. You're probably glad that God created you! There are surely other parts of creation you love and enjoy: people, for instance, and horses and dogs and dolphins. If you appreciate any of those, you're appreciating God's creation. And who doesn't like food? All food comes to us, if we trace it back far enough, from God's creation.

Almost everyone is a nature lover to some degree. But the Bible tells us there are wrong ways and a right way to love nature. The Bible tells us that the crowning point of God's creation was people. God made people able to appreciate all the rest of his creation so that people would praise and worship God for it. God knew this was what would make people happier than anything else—seeing how wonderful he is and praising him for it. God intended creation to reveal to people his greatness.

But the first people sinned. They obeyed Satan (a creature) in the form of a serpent (another creature), instead of obeying the Creator. From then on, every member of the human race has been born sinful. Every member of the human race chooses to trade the worship of the Creator for the worship of creation.

Some people worship creation by praying to created things, like stars and rocks. Some people worship creation by living to enjoy created things instead of living to enjoy God. Some people make themselves (creatures) the center of their own universe, so that they are their own idols. There are many different ways we do it, but all people, left to themselves, find some way to worship what God made instead of worshiping God.

Of course, it should be different with God's people. Their hearts have been changed. God has turned them from idols to serve the living and true God (1 Thess. 1:9). God has opened the eyes of his people to the truth they could never see before. So God's people should look at creation with new eyes and love it with pure hearts. God's people love God's creation because they see the revelation of God himself in it.

Creation, or "general revelation," cannot take the place of God's written Word, or "special revelation." God's written Word, the Bible, gives many precise details about who God is, how he saves his people, and what he wants of them. Still, when a believer sees the wonderful things God has created, he enjoys it more than an unbeliever can, because he sees something of God in it. *I know the Person who made this,* he thinks when he watches a beautiful sunset. *And that Person is truly amazing!*

As for me and my house . . .

- Did you know that many famous scientists in history were Christians who studied science because it enabled them to see how wonderfully God works in his creation?

- How many different things can you think of that people live for instead of God? How is each of those a "created thing"?

- Even Christians are tempted to serve idols rather than God. What particular created things are the most tempting to you?

Take Off Your Shoes!

God Reveals Himself through His Creation

"Holy, holy, holy, is the LORD of hosts; the whole earth is full of his glory!"
Isaiah 6:3

> *Earth's crammed with heaven,*
> *And every common bush afire with God;*
> *And only he who sees takes off his shoes;*
> *The rest sit around it and pluck blackberries.*
> Elizabeth Barrett Browning (from "Aurora Leigh")

E arth's crammed with heaven." Earth is full of things that constantly remind us of God. The Bible uses many illustrations from creation. God is a rock. Jesus is a vine. The Holy Spirit is like the wind. It isn't that God looks around at what he has made, thinking, *Hmm. What could I use to illustrate my holiness?* I know! I'll use light! Rather, God created the light as something he would use to help us understand his perfect, sinless nature. God built into the universe many such things to help us know him better.

"And every common bush [is] afire with God." Of course, you know when a bush actually was on fire with God. It was when God spoke to Moses from the burning bush. The author of the poem above is saying that every created thing is like that burning bush in a way, because God uses even common, ordinary things to announce to us something of his greatness and glory.

But, according to our poet, that's only true for *some* people. "Only he who sees takes off his shoes." When Moses heard God speak from the burning bush, God told him, "Take off your shoes. You're standing on holy ground." The poet is telling us, that in one sense, all creation is holy ground.

All creation should cause us to stop and take notice of God, because everything in it reveals something of God to us. Some people see what created things show us about God, and they "take off their shoes." They worship God and give him glory for what they see of him in what he has made.

The poet calls this kind of person someone "who sees." "The rest" of people, she says, have a different response to nature. When they see a bush, they don't think of God at all, so they don't worship. "The rest sit around it and pluck blackberries." All that these people see in creation is what it's in it for them. They may enjoy looking at the moon because they find it beautiful. They may enjoy swimming in the lake because it's fun. They may enjoy eating the food that comes from plants, or they may have a business and use creation to make money. They enjoy God's creation for all these reasons, but they never let it lead them to worship. They don't "see" God and his attributes in what he has made.

Even Christians take creation for granted and fail to notice God's revelation in it. In this book, we will practice "seeing." We'll consider each thing God made during the creation week, looking to see how it shows us something of who God is. But because creation is only "general revelation" and limited, we will also look at God's "special revelation," his Word, to see how God himself said these created things teach us of him. Our goal will be to develop the habit of looking at creation and "seeing" reminders of God, so that we'll take off our shoes and worship God for who he is and what he has done.

As for me and my house . . .

- Brainstorm as many created things as you can think of in thirty seconds. When the time is up, ask yourself what each of these created things shows us to be true about God. Do you know a place in Scripture where any of these things are used to illustrate something?

Day 1

Light and Water

No Darkness at All
The Holiness of God

*"This is the message we have heard from him and proclaim to you,
that God is light, and in him is no darkness at all."*
1 John 1:5

Because God made people in his own image, people can create all kinds of things. They compose music, build huge skyscrapers, bake exquisite chocolate cookies, and carve wood into beautiful shapes. Of course, if they're going to make things well, they must first learn how and then practice. And they must have materials to use. God, the Creator of the universe, made all that is from nothing, and he made it simply by speaking.

The first words we see God speaking are, "Let there be light" (Gen. 1:3). As soon as God said this, the Bible tells us, there was light. God separated the light from the darkness, and God considered the light that he had made to be good.

When someone has a wicked plan in mind—he wants to steal a wallet or break into a house—he seldom does it in broad daylight because, if people see him, they will stop him. If he has a "dark" deed to do, he waits for darkness in which to do it. He hides in a shadow in a poorly lit street and watches for an unsuspecting passerby. Or he finds a window on the dark side of a house to break for his robbery. For this reason, we associate darkness with evil.

Imagine you're opening a door into a dark room you've never seen before, and you can't find the light switch. You enter carefully because, just maybe, someone's hiding in there. Now imagine that you're opening an-

16

other door, and you find a bright room with every light on. You march right in, without a second thought.

The Bible tells us that God is light. There is not the slightest speck of darkness anywhere in him. In our key verse, God is using light to help us understand his perfect moral purity. He is only good and holy, never bad or evil. In fact, the Bible tells us that God is "of purer eyes than to see evil and cannot look at wrong" (Hab. 1:13). This is why God demands over and over in the Old and New Testaments that his people be holy—because he is holy. We cannot "have fellowship with him" and "walk in darkness" (1 John 1:6).

Then what shall we do, because none of us is holy? All of us sin. All of us think, say, and do what is evil even when we try very hard not to. God sent his Son for this very reason. When we confess that we are sinners and trust in Christ as the One who took our sin's punishment on the cross, God cleanses us of our sin. Then we can walk in the light with our holy, sinless God (1 John 1:7–9).

As for me and my house . . .

- Read some of the stories where we see people coming face-to-face with the light of God's holiness and realizing they live in darkness: Isaiah (Isa. 6:1–7); Ezekiel (Ezek. 1:26–2:7, 3:12–15); Peter (Luke 5:1–11); John (Rev. 1:12–18); rebellious sinners (Rev. 6:12–17).

- John wrote a letter to Christians so they could enjoy fellowship with God. Read the first chapter of 1 John and explain it in your own words.

Light for Life

Jesus Is the Light of the World

"Again Jesus spoke to them, saying, 'I am the light of the world. . . .'"
John 8:12

"In him was life, and the life was the light of men."
John 1:4

Have you ever conducted a science project where you demonstrated under what conditions plants grow best? Some plants you may have fed and watered regularly; other plants you neglected. For some plants, you may have played Mozart's music; for others, heavy metal. Another thing you might have tried was growing some plants where there was plenty of light and others in a dark closet.

If you tried this last experiment, you discovered that plants cannot grow without light. The plants you tried to maintain in darkness probably turned yellow, and eventually brown or black. If you continued the experiment long enough, the plants finally died.

Light is one of those things we take for granted, but it is a basic ingredient for life. Plants must have light or they will die, and all other forms of life depend on plants. So if there were no light, there would be no life.

Jesus knew there can be no life without light when he claimed to be the Light of the World. He knew that, without him, no one can live. Adam chose to eat a piece of fruit in disobedience to God, and, in that day, Adam died as God had said he would. Adam's body did not drop dead on the spot, although it began to age and deteriorate, but he became spiritually dead. The part of him made to know, love, and enjoy God died. Adam passed on that spiritual death to all of us.

Apart from Christ, we all live in a dark kingdom of dead people. We are like the plants in the closet. We do not have what we need for life, and there is no way we can get it. The Lord Jesus Christ burst into our dark world as a blaze of glorious, life-giving light. He had what we needed to begin to live.

Because Jesus is God the Son, when he was born as a human, he was born sinless. He had no darkness and no death in him. He lived a life of perfect obedience to God, earning every spiritual blessing there is. All that obedience to God is counted as ours, when our faith is in Jesus to save us. Jesus died an undeserved death on a cross, taking on himself the wrath of God that his people deserved. Those who are united to Christ are no longer in darkness and death. They have been placed in the light and in life.

When Paul wrote to fellow believers in Colossae, he told them God had qualified them to share "in the inheritance of the saints in light." He said God "has delivered us from the domain of darkness and transferred us to the kingdom of his beloved Son" (Col. 1:12–13). It is as though God has lifted us, like dead plants, from the dark closet and put us on the windowsill, in the bright light of Christ, where we have what we need to live and grow.

As for me and my house . . .

- If you've never tried the plant experiment, try it to see how necessary light is for life.

- Notice the plants in your home. Which way does the new growth on them face? Plants "understand" they must have light to live, and they grow toward it.

- If you have any new plants or flowers coming up in your yard, consider how dark it was underground and see how the plants push their way through all that dirt to get out into the light.

Light up the Night!

The Holy Spirit's Illumination of a Sinner's Heart

*"For God, who said, 'Let light shine out of darkness,' has shone
in our hearts to give the light of the knowledge of the glory
of God in the face of Jesus Christ."*

2 Corinthians 4:6

You and I are in a hallway with no windows. The only light is from the electric light overhead. We come to the doorway of a room you have never seen. I turn off the hall light, then I open the door. All is pitch black. "There's a fifty-dollar bill on the table in there," I say, "and it's yours. But hurry, we don't have much time." Of course, you're eager to have the fifty-dollar bill. But you don't hurry too fast, because you have no idea what's in the room. You proceed cautiously, feeling your way. You find that the room is large and full of furniture. Not only that, but there are many things on the floor you could step on or trip over. You spend several minutes trying to find the table with the money on it, but you get nowhere. At last, you feel a light switch on the wall. You flick it, and instantly everything is crystal clear to you. There's the table, over behind a couch. You swiftly step over or around the things in your way, snatch the bill, and are ready to go.

Have you ever wondered how non-Christians can hear the gospel presented very clearly and pay no attention? They have just heard their sinful hearts described, they have heard what God will do to judge sin, and they have heard how he has graciously provided a Savior—and all they want to do is go get lunch!

Unbelievers can't see all those clear truths because their hearts are darkened by sin (Rom. 1:21). Not only that, but Satan has "blinded the

minds of the unbelievers, to keep them from seeing the light of the gospel . . ."
(2 Cor. 4:4). The furniture and all the things on the floor are there, but they can't see them, so they can't navigate around them. Hearts are sinful; God judges sin; there is a Savior. But unbelievers can't see these things, so they don't act accordingly.

The Bible tells us that God illumines the darkness of a sinner's heart when he calls that person to repent and trust in Christ. It is as though God flicks a switch and the darkness of a person's heart is flooded with light. Suddenly, the person sees what was there all along. He understands what was always true but what never made sense to him before.

God uses light to show us how wonderful he is. When we stand outside on a sunny day, we can remember that our God is light, having not the least shadow of evil. When we see plants growing toward the sun, we can remember that Jesus is the light of the world and the only one who can give spiritual life. And when we turn on a light so that we can see what we need to see, we can be grateful for how the Holy Spirit shines into the hearts of his people, driving away the spiritual darkness that had always blinded them before.

As for me and my house . . .

- Read these accounts of different reactions to the gospel. Those who received it were those whose hearts God had illumined: Acts 4:1–4; 13:43–45, 48–49; 17:10–13, 32–34; 19:8–10, 18–20; 28:23–24.

- Praise God for: creating light with just his word; being light—being perfectly holy; giving Jesus, the life-giving Light of the World; shining into the hearts of his people so they understand the gospel.

6

God Owns the Light

The Ninth Plague

Exodus 10:21–29

"Have you commanded the morning since your days began,
and caused the dawn to know its place . . . ?
Where is the way to the dwelling of light,
and where is the place of darkness . . . ?"

Job 38:12, 19

Nighttime brings darkness. Morning brings the light. Everyone knows that. Then why, in the middle of the day, had it grown pitch dark? It wasn't dark like it gets on a cloudy day or when a huge dust cloud blows up from the desert, blotting out the sun. In those cases, the sun is obscured, but it still sends some light through, and people can see. This darkness was absolute, like the darkness in a cave deep underground when no one has a flashlight. This was darkness you could feel. This darkness had not come gradually, as it does when the sun sets. Suddenly, in an instant in the middle of the day, light was gone. The Egyptians could have held their hands right in front of their faces and not seen the faintest outline of them.

What had happened? The God who owns the light, who gives it commands and is always obeyed, had told Moses, "Stretch out your hand toward heaven, that there may be darkness over the land of Egypt, a darkness to be felt" (Ex. 10:21). Moses had done as God had said, and this pitch darkness was the result.

The darkness lasted three days. Three days that must have felt like three years to the Egyptians! If you've ever toured a cave and had the guide turn off the lights to show you how dark it is, you might have begun to feel a little nervous after just a few seconds of being able to see absolutely nothing. Imagine three days of pitch dark!

Nothing was wrong with the sun, however. The Israelite slaves, who lived in their own section of Egypt called Goshen, had light during the daytime just like they always did. God was selective about where he sent this terrible darkness.

God sent the darkness because Pharaoh stubbornly refused to obey his Creator. God wanted his people freed from slavery and sent out of Egypt, but Pharaoh had foolishly replied that *he* didn't know this God; why should *he* do what this God said? So God set out to show him who he was. He sent eight other plagues before this one, and would send yet one more. God's will would be done; sooner or later, it always is.

This particular plague especially mocked Pharaoh. The Egyptians believed that Pharaoh was one with the sun god, Ra. The sun's most important job, of course, was to provide light for the land of Egypt. God had commanded darkness, instead of light, and there was not a thing the pharaoh could do about it. The darkness lasted precisely as long as God commanded it to, and light did not return until God allowed.

Most of the time, light comes with the dawn, as God has ordained. When God wants to, however, he can change that. He made light, and it belongs to him. He can do with it whatever he wishes.

As for me and my house . . .

- God asked Job the questions in the key verses to show Job how much more God knows than humans know and how much more he can do than humans can do. When it's dark, God knows where the light is. When it's light, God knows where he keeps the dark. God commands the morning. Light and dark belong to God, and both obey him.

7

Measuring the Ocean and Commanding the Waves

The Greatness of God

"O Lord God of hosts,
who is mighty as you are, O Lord,
with your faithfulness all around you?
You rule the raging of the sea;
when its waves rise, you still them."

Psalm 89:8–9

I magine that you woke one morning to find that, overnight, all the water in the world had disappeared. Rivers, oceans, and swimming pools were empty; faucets were dry. If there were no water, of course, all the fish would die, and it would not be long before plants, animals, and humans would disappear as well. All life depends on water. Perhaps that's one reason why God created it first.

Genesis 1:2 tells us that even before God said, "Let there be light," his Spirit "was hovering over the face of the waters." The Bible doesn't describe God's creation of water, but since he made all that is, we can be sure he created water too.

The oceans contain most of the water God created, but there are also long rivers, wide seas, and large lakes. If you were to add up all that water, how much would there be? To measure water for a recipe, you'd use a measuring cup. To measure water for mixing cement, you'd use a gallon bucket. To measure water for a construction project, you'd use the tank on the back of a big truck. What container would possibly hold enough water to measure all the water on earth? Isaiah 40:12 describes God as the one who "has measured the waters in the hollow of his hand."

Oceans cover nearly three-fourths of the earth's surface. Although man has explored, charted, and learned to travel on them, they remain mysterious and powerful in ways that dwarf human beings. In Scripture, God uses the greatness of the oceans to show us how much greater he is than we can even imagine.

Modern technology enables us to build sturdy ships and to avoid storms at sea, but we cannot control the ocean and its weather. God can, though. With all our exploring, there are many places deep under the ocean's surface that man has never visited or even measured. Job 38:16 describes God as the one who has "entered into the springs of the sea" and "walked in the recesses of the deep."

Ocean waves are powerful and strong. Yet they never flood all the land, not even at high tide. When you walk along the beach, the waves come in and tickle your toes, but they always go back out again. Waves pound some coasts with violence, day and night, but on every ocean coast there is a certain point beyond which the waves never come. That's because God set limits for the ocean waves when he made them. Speaking about the sea, God told Job that he had "prescribed limits for it and set bars and doors, and said, 'Thus far shall you come, and no farther, and here shall your proud waves be stayed'" (Job 38:10–11).

When we stand at the ocean's edge, gazing on water stretching farther than we can see and listening to the pounding of the powerful waves, we should feel awe at the greatness of the God who created and rules this vast, powerful, mysterious world of water.

As for me and my house . . .

- If you live near an ocean, plan a trip to the coast with the specific purpose of seeing the greatness of God in what he has made and worshiping him for it.

- Do some research to gather amazing facts about the ocean for the purpose of giving God glory for what he has done.

God Owns the Water

An Axe Head Floats

2 Kings 6:1–7

"Whatever the LORD pleases, he does,
in heaven and on earth,
in the seas and all deeps."

Psalm 135:6

God not only created everything that is, he is also the Lord of everything that is. When he created the world, he made certain rules for each thing he made, and all things obey his rules, always. Because God is their Lord, though, God can cause created things to behave differently than they normally do. Whenever he chooses, God can interrupt the rules he gave his creation.

When God made water, he made rules for it. One rule is that water cannot hold its own shape. If I pour a cup of water into a pile on the tabletop, it will not stay in a pile. It will run all over the table and flow down onto the floor. Another rule for water is that it won't hold things up. Unless something is very lightweight or has a special design, that thing will sink if I try to set it on water.

Elisha was a prophet in Old Testament times. As a prophet, Elisha's task was to communicate God's word to his people. Since people needed to know that Elisha spoke with God's own authority, God gave Elisha the power to perform miracles.

Elisha taught and led other men who were also prophets—so many, in fact, that there wasn't room for them all in the place where they lived. One of them suggested that they build a larger home. Elisha agreed. Before people can build, of course, they need something to build with. In this case, the builders would use wood. Since ancient Israel had no lumberyards, the men headed for a place near the river where they could cut trees for the lumber they needed. One man had no axe to use, so he went to the home of a friend and borrowed an axe. He promised to take good care of the axe and to return it when he was finished.

As this particular man worked, cutting trees with everyone else and then cutting the trees into pieces to use for building, the head of his axe—the sharp, metal part that cuts into the wood—began to loosen from the handle. With each stroke, the axe head became looser, until finally it flew off the handle and through the air, landing—splash!—in the river. The axe head, being made of heavy iron, obeyed God's rules and fell straight to the bottom of the water.

Horrified, the man cried out to Elisha, "Alas, my master! It was borrowed!" How could he return it if it was deep at the bottom of the river?

Elisha hurried over. "Where did it fall?" he asked. The man pointed. There was no axe head to be seen. Elisha cut a small piece of wood and put it in the water where the axe head had sunk. Of course, the wood floated. But floating wood doesn't cause iron to float—at least, not usually. God is the Lord of water and of iron, though, and Elisha's floating wood caused the axe head to float up to the surface, where the thankful man could snatch it up and reattach it tightly to the handle.

As for me and my house . . .

- Spend some time considering what would happen if water didn't obey God's rules for it. What if sometimes water flowed from your spigot, but sometimes it didn't? What if sometimes water flowed downhill from mountains, filling lakes, but sometimes flowed back up? Thank God for his wise rules for creation.

- What other Bible stories can you think of where God caused water to behave differently than it normally does?

Coming Clean

A Fountain for Cleansing

"If we confess our sins, he is faithful and just to forgive us
our sins and to cleanse us from all unrighteousness."

1 John 1:9

Y ou've been out running on a warm day and perspiration runs down from your hair and into your eyes. Your clothes are soaked with sweat. What do you really want to do right now? Jump in a swimming pool and rinse off all that sweat!

Your little brother just bumped your hand and the glass of soda you held splashed all over your favorite shirt. What do you want to do immediately? Pull off the shirt and rinse it in the sink.

You've been camping in the woods for days with limited water, and you're beginning to smell bad! Once you finally get home, what's the first thing you want to do? Jump in the shower, of course.

When you're really dirty, plenty of clean water is just what you need. But what kind of water works on our deepest filth, and where will we find enough of it? The Bible tells us that the human heart is so filthy from sin that God can't stand it. It disgusts him. Nothing we can do can change that. We cannot cleanse our hearts. We're hopeless before the uncleanness of our sin.

One of God's many gracious promises to his Old Testament people was this one: "I will sprinkle clean water on you, and you shall be clean from all your uncleannesses . . ." (Ezek. 36:25). The clean water God would sprinkle them with would be able to remove even their deepest dirt.

But would there be enough to go around, for all the people of God who need clean hearts? Another Old Testament promise is: "On that day there shall be a fountain opened for the house of David and the inhabitants of Jerusalem, to cleanse them from sin and uncleanness" (Zech. 13:1). Not just a basin, not just a tank—God would open a whole fountain that would flow until every last spot of sin was cleansed from God's people. "That day" was the time of God's promised Messiah. It was in Jesus that God opened this purifying fountain.

Most of us don't think of it often enough, but by far the greatest need of every human being is to be cleansed from sin. God hates sin so much and will judge and punish it severely. In his amazing grace, God has given us just what we need to be pure and clean before him. We must be sure to take advantage of what he has provided. The blood of his own Son, poured out on the cross as he was judged in the place of God's people, is the only thing that can cleanse us from sin.

We need to admit the filthiness of our hearts and stop trying to clean them up on our own. We must come for cleansing to the fountain God provides in Christ. We'll get "dirty" again, every day, many times! Yet every time we sin, we will find the fountain still flowing, still just as effective as it was on the day it was first opened.

As for me and my house . . .

- Consider God's wonderful invitation to "come clean" in these verses: Isaiah 1:18; Psalm 51:1–2; 1 John 1:9.
- Try to let some of the many times that you wash daily remind you of the wonderful cleansing available in the Lord Jesus Christ that removes the worst dirt of all.

Can't Live without It!

Jesus and the Woman at the Well

John 4:1–41

"Jesus said to her, 'Everyone who drinks of this water will be thirsty again, but whoever drinks of the water that I will give him will never be thirsty again. The water that I will give him will become in him a spring of water welling up to eternal life.'"

John 4:13–14

The woman peered out at the dusty road. It shimmered in the heat of the noonday sun. She dreaded the thought of toting the heavy water jar all the way to the well and then lugging it, full, back home again. She had waited long past the cool of the morning, when all the other women had gone, and she could wait no longer. All the water in the house was gone, and she was thirsty. She sighed, lifted the jar to her shoulder, and slipped out the door.

The woman walked slowly, to keep as cool as possible. Her eagerness for a drink drew her, as she remembered the fresh, clear water deep in the well. As she drew near it, the woman's heart sank. She had waited all this time and come in the heat of the day so she would meet no one on her way. Yet someone sat there, all alone, beside the well.

When she got to the well, though, the woman knew she was safe. The man was a Jew. She was a Samaritan. He would never speak to her. She dropped the bucket down deep into the well, waited for it to fill, pulled it back up, and poured the cool, clear water into her jar.

"Give me a drink," the man said. Startled though she was, the woman no doubt gave him a drink. He was clearly hot and weary. Yet she had to ask: "How is it that you, a Jew, ask for a drink from me, a woman of Samaria?"

Nothing could have prepared the woman for the man's reply. "If you knew the gift of God, and who it is that is saying to you, 'Give me a drink,' you would have asked him, and he would have given you living water."

"You don't even have a bucket!" the woman said. "Where do you get this living water?"

"Everyone who drinks of this water will be thirsty again, but whoever drinks of the water that I will give him will never be thirsty again," Jesus—for that's who the man was—told her. He went on to show the woman that he was the Messiah God had promised to send. He talked with her about the sinful past that kept her anxious to avoid people, and the woman believed in him.

God built into every human body a need for water. He also built into every human soul a need for himself. Our sin prevents this need from being met, but Jesus came to deal with our sin and to give us living water. Our bodies can't live without water. In the same way, we have no spiritual life without the living water Jesus gives. On a hot day, nothing tastes as delicious to a thirsty throat as a glass of cold water. In the same way, nothing in heaven or earth is as enjoyable as knowing God. Jesus alone can give us the living water that truly satisfies and that lasts forever.

As for me and my house . . .

- Can you remember a time when you were desperately thirsty and had to wait before getting a drink of water? With that feeling in mind, read Psalm 42:1–2.

- Read John 7:37–39, Isaiah 55:1, and Revelation 22:17. These verses give further examples of Jesus' provision and gracious invitation.

Water in the Desert

God's Surprising Grace

*"I will open rivers on the bare heights,
    and fountains in the midst of the valleys.
I will make the wilderness a pool of water,
    and the dry land springs of water."*

Isaiah 41:18

They had been without water before. Only three days after leaving Egypt, the Israelites had finally arrived, weary and thirsty, at the first water they'd seen on the trip, only to discover that it was bad water and not drinkable. God had provided for them then, just as he'd provided safety from the plagues and escape from the Egyptian army. They had panicked first, though. They had grumbled against Moses and failed to trust God. But God had shown Moses a log to throw into the bad water, which had made it perfectly good, and they'd had all they needed.

Here the Israelites were again, though, on this same journey to the Promised Land, with the same problem—and they were responding in the same way. They were in the wilderness, precisely where God had told them to go, but there was no water. The people quarreled with Moses and complained that they'd been better off in Egypt. God told Moses to strike a rock with his rod, and water gushed forth, plenty for all the thousands of people and their animals.

A desert receives ten inches (or less) of rainfall a year. That's not very much! Because deserts usually have high temperatures, what rainfall does occur evaporates quickly, leaving no lakes or even little ponds. Since water is so essential for life, travel across a desert can be a dangerous thing. It was not dangerous, though, for the Israelites, because God was with them, directing exactly where they were to go. He knew they had to have water, and he provided it all along the way.

Water in the desert is a complete surprise. God uses it in Scripture as a picture of the unexpected miracles he works in salvation. After reminding his people of how he had led them out of Egypt, God promised them, through Isaiah, "Behold, I am doing a new thing; now it springs forth, do you not perceive it? I will make a way in the wilderness and rivers in the desert" (Isa. 43:19).

How likely is water in a desert? How likely is it that the Spirit of the holy God would live in a sinful human being? How likely is it that God would bless those who deserved his curse for their sin? Yet God promised, through the prophet Isaiah, "I will pour water on the thirsty land, and streams on the dry ground; I will pour my Spirit upon your offspring and my blessing on your descendants" (Isa. 44:3).

How likely is it that the skies will dump rain on the desert? And if they do, how likely is it that the rain will soak into the desert floor, resulting in plants growing, flourishing, and producing fruit? How likely is it that people who have always chosen sin will be righteous and produce fruit that pleases God? Yet God described the future he had for his people in Christ: "Shower, O heavens, from above, and let the clouds rain down righteousness; let the earth open that salvation and righteousness may bear fruit . . ." (Isa. 45:8).

The grace of God, poured out on sinners and making them righteous, is a greater surprise than a waterfall tumbling down into deep pools in the desert!

As for me and my house . . .

- What are some "surprise" conversions you can think of, either in Bible stories or in the lives of people you know or have read about? (Consider Zacchaeus or Saul in the New Testament, or Rahab or Naaman in the Old.)

Acquiring a Taste

Living Water? Or Broken Storage Tanks?

"For my people have committed two evils:
they have forsaken me,
*   the fountain of living waters,*
and hewed out cisterns for themselves,
*   broken cisterns that can hold no water."*

Jeremiah 2:13

When Jesus told the woman at the well that he could give her "living water," he was making a play on words. "Living" water is water coming from a spring or a rushing stream. Because it's always moving, "living water" doesn't become stagnant or collect debris, insects, and scum. The woman's well water was good, coming as it did from deep underground, but it wasn't "living" water. "Living" water would have been better. Of course, Jesus' deeper meaning in "living water" was that he could provide what would give eternal life to our souls.

If you lived in a desert and had no spring or stream for living water, you would dig a well to get at the groundwater. And if that didn't work, you would make for yourself a cistern. A cistern was a hole in the ground, walled in, for the purpose of collecting any rainwater that might fall.

In Jeremiah 2, where we find our key verse, God becomes angry with Old Testament Israel's idolatry. Though they had known the true and living God and had seen his miracles on their behalf, the Israelites had turned to the idols of the neighboring nations. This was not only wicked; it was foolish.

Imagine people who have a fountain in the back yard that gushes pure, clear spring water. "We don't want that water," these people say. Instead, they dig a cistern, where the best they will be able to get will be murky, dirty water that smells bad. Not only that, but they make a broken cistern, so full of cracks that any rain falling into it will leak right out again. What fools! Turning from God to idols is like abandoning a fountain of living water to make a broken cistern that won't hold water. You just won't get what you need that way!

The sin of the human heart is such that people turn first to created things, instead of to the true God, for security and joy. Primitive peoples pray to trees and rocks and animals to care for them. "Civilized" peoples find their happiness in having many possessions and trusting them to meet their needs. Religious people may have ideas that make them feel secure and happy, but if those ideas don't agree with the Bible's teaching, the ideas are idols.

This foolish and wicked choice of created things instead of God is so natural to sinners that even Christians must always keep watch over their hearts. "Little children," the apostle John wrote to a church full of Christians, "keep yourselves from idols" (1 John 5:21). God has given us a book filled with stories of his protection for his people and with promises that he will always provide all they need and more. Time spent in God's Word, seeing who he is and what he does, will produce in us a taste for living water. We should ask God daily to help us see how wonderful he is, to show us how limited are other things we might trust or enjoy, and to keep us from preferring idols to him.

As for me and my house . . .

- Think of something that makes you very happy. Think of something you feel you couldn't live without. Those things could become (or maybe are) idols for you. Make a list of all the ways in which God is better than those things and can meet your needs where those things cannot.

Day 3

Land and Plants

Measuring the Land

How Great Is Our God!

"For the Lord is a great God,
and a great King above all gods.
In his hand are the depths of the earth;
the heights of the mountains are his also."

Psalm 95:3–4

Water is wonderful! We couldn't live without it. But what if our planet contained nothing but water? We still couldn't live, and neither could many other creatures. The Bible tells us that on the third day of creation, God commanded all the waters to gather together into one place so the dry land could appear.

We can learn much about God when we stop and really *see* the land he made, in all its different forms. The tallest mountains tower so high that at their tops the air is too thin to breathe. A canyon, the opposite of a mountain, drops off thousands of feet between its rim and its floor. The Bible tells us, as a way of describing God's greatness, that he holds both the depths of the earth and the heights of the mountains in his hand.

What is a mountain made of? It's made of many tiny pieces of rock, or even finer grains of sand, or even smaller pieces of dust. How many pieces of rock, sand, and dust would be found in just one mountain? What if you added them together, then mixed in all the dust from the rest of earth's land as well? How much would there be? How much would all that weigh? The Bible tells us that God "enclosed the dust of the earth in a measure and weighed the mountains in scales and the hills in a balance" (Isa. 40:12).

A tall mountain peak is majestic and imposing, all by itself. Almost every mountain peak, though, is simply one peak in a whole range of mountains. Some mountain ranges spread for miles across whole continents. Mountains can be massive, which is why they are symbols of strength and permanence. They don't move. While they do change because of forces of wind and water, they change so slowly that a photograph of a mountain taken fifty years ago usually appears no different than the picture of the same mountain taken yesterday. As strong as mountains are, how much stronger is "the one who by his strength established the mountains, being girded with might" (Ps. 65:6)?

The prophet Amos says this of God: "For behold, he who forms the mountains and creates the wind, and declares to man what is his thought, who makes the morning darkness, and treads on the heights of the earth—the LORD, the God of hosts, is his name!" (Amos 4:13). In ancient times, sometimes a king or general who had conquered a city or a land would make a victory march up to its highest point. This symbolized that the place now belonged to him. It was under his rule. God treads on the highest places of the earth. The whole earth belongs to him and is under his rule.

God has built into us all a sense of awe when we look up at the clouds covering a high mountain peak or when we gaze down into the depths of a canyon. That sense of awe is meant to call us to marvel at the greatness of our God, to "take off our shoes," and to worship.

As for me and my house . . .

- Remember with your family high mountains or deep canyons that you've seen together. Watch a nature movie about mountains or canyons with your family and praise God together for the wonder of what he's made and for his greatness.

Who Will Live Where?

Geography, Nations, and the Sovereignty of God

*"And he made from one man every nation of mankind to
live on all the face of the earth, having determined allotted
periods and the boundaries of their dwelling place."*

Acts 17:26

Geography matters! The land that provides a home for a nation has great influence on what that nation becomes. When you read history, you learn that democracy had its beginning in Greece—Athens to be specific. Because of the water and the mountains separating ancient Greeks from each other, Greeks lived in city-states, governments small enough for all citizens to be involved in state decisions. Greece's geography was one of the reasons democracy could flourish in Athens and become a guiding ideal for Western civilization.

Rome, partway down the "boot" of Italy, was protected on one side by a long chain of mountains. It was inland far enough to be safe from attack by sea, yet had easy access for travel to that same sea via the Tiber River. From their geography, ancient Romans had what they needed to grow strong and secure in their own home, while being able to travel all over the Mediterranean to reach other lands to conquer and rule.

If you look on a world map for the tiny little land of Israel, you will find that it sits on a sort of land bridge connecting three continents: Africa, Asia, and Europe. The early church, begun in Jerusalem, was in exactly the best spot to be a center from which the gospel could go out to all nations.

When God created land where people could live, he didn't form one giant rectangular piece of land surrounded by the earth's oceans. Instead, he created continents and islands and peninsulas and all sorts of interesting land masses. Some lands have miles of smooth coastlines, making sea travel easy for their citizens as well as making them open to conquerors in boats. Some lands are bordered by mountains difficult to cross, protecting the inhabitants and isolating them from new ideas or the influence of others. Some lands are well watered, resulting in easy lives of plenty with leisure to develop great civilizations. In other lands, hardly anything will grow, and people stay busy simply surviving.

Was it just by chance that certain people settled in certain places? Or did someone decide which people would live where?

The Bible teaches that God rules the history of mankind and of each individual nation. He raises up and brings down kings. He prospers certain nations, enabling them to influence and even rule other nations. As we watch some people come to power and some nations grow strong, we usually don't know what God intends to accomplish, but we can be sure he has purposes in all these things, and that he always works to bring those purposes to pass.

One way in which God works in the lives of nations and in the history of our world is through geography. The Bible tells us that God is the one who formed all lands and who decided which peoples would live in which lands. He divided mankind and fixed their boundaries (Deut. 32:8). He rules rulers, partly through the land he created.

As for me and my house . . .

- Look through an atlas, noticing different geographical features that could make a difference in how people in different areas would live. Look up specific countries online or in history books and notice that their geography is always described. Notice how often it seems to influence the country's history. Praise God for his sovereign rule in deciding who would live where all over our planet.

Mountains and a Rock
God as Eternal and Unchanging

"Lord, you have been our dwelling place
in all generations.
Before the mountains were brought forth,
or ever you had formed the earth and the world,
from everlasting to everlasting you are God." Psalm 90:1–2

"On God rests my salvation and my glory;
my mighty rock, my refuge is God." Psalm 62:7

Hannibal led his entire army, complete with elephants, from Carthage in North Africa over the Alps in Italy to attack Rome. The Romans were sure he couldn't do it, because the Alps are so high and rugged, but Hannibal succeeded. If you ever go to Italy, you can see the same Alps Hannibal crossed. There may be some slight changes, but even though it's been thousands of years, the mountains remain basically the same as they were in Hannibal's day.

Mountains don't die. They don't go away. They stand as symbols of stability and changelessness. Our mountains today are older than any other created thing. God, of course, is older, for God is eternal. Moses wrote Psalm 90. He began it by rejoicing that the people of God have had God forever. One generation dies and a new generation replaces it. Change after change occurs. But God remains the eternal dwelling place of his people. He has always been. He always will be. He never changes.

Mountains are made of rock. Scripture often compares God to a rock, which is stable and sure. When you hike on a steep slope, you won't put your foot on the loose gravel and sand, because it slips out from under your boot. You could end up sliding down the mountain as part of an avalanche! You try to step from solid rock to solid rock, because a rock won't slip out from under you. You can trust a rock. Scripture says of God, "Trust in the LORD forever, for the LORD GOD is an everlasting rock" (Isa. 26:4).

People build houses on rock so the foundations won't wash away in floods. In ancient times, people built fortresses in the rock. They were hard for enemies to reach, and they provided sure, solid, fireproof protection from arrows and spears. The psalmists often compared God to a rock and a refuge, a place of safety for his people. Of course, that's not to say that with God as our rock, nothing hurtful or unpleasant will ever touch us. If God is our rock, nothing can cause us ultimate harm. Our rock will keep our souls for heaven and, if our bodies die before Jesus returns, he will raise them new and strong.

When you step outside your house, you probably seldom worry that the ground will move away from under your foot. You count on the ground to stay where it is. We expect the earth to remain right where it is in our galaxy, with all its land remaining firm. That is only the case, though, because that is what God has decreed. "The LORD reigns," wrote the psalmist, "he is robed in majesty; the LORD is robed; he has put on strength as his belt. Yes, the world is established; it shall never be moved" (Ps. 93:1).

That's how it is now, and that's how it will be as long as God holds all things together. The day will come, though, God has promised, when "the earth will wear out like a garment, and they who dwell in it will die in like manner; but my salvation will be forever . . ." (Isa. 51:6). God is the eternal rock of his people, longer lasting than the mountains, surer than the most solid of rocks. Our trust can never be misplaced when we have placed it in him.

As for me and my house . . .

• Pray for people you know who are struggling with difficulties and ask God to help them trust him in their trials. Pray for God's persecuted people in other lands, asking God to help them be aware of the strong and lasting refuge he is to them.

Surrounded by Mountains

God as Our Sure Protector

*"Those who trust in the L*ORD *are like Mount Zion,*
which cannot be moved, but abides forever.
As the mountains surround Jerusalem,
*so the L*ORD *surrounds his people,*
from this time forth and forevermore."

Psalm 125:1–2

I swallowed the last bite of my after-school snack and darted out the front door. I hurried up my street and crossed the highway at the end of it, heading for the three small desert hills on the other side. The first hill had a home and a small business on it; I had broken my arm once on that hill. The other two hills were lonely places, crisscrossed by paths on which I sometimes met coyotes.

I loved those three hills when I was growing up and climbed them often. I loved the wide open view from the hills, across the desert and to the mountains in the distance. To the east was Superstition Mountain, the center of many local legends about lost gold mines and murders. To the north was the one we called "Scarface" because of the line across the front of it. In the west, on an Indian reservation, was Red Mountain, named for its distinctive red rock. Camelback lay to the west, South Mountain to the south, and, in between were many other mountain ranges I couldn't name. I could turn all the way around, there on my hill, and see an unbroken circle of mountains. It made me feel secure to always see the same mountains, completely surrounding my desert valley.

When I read our key verse ("As the mountains surround Jerusalem, so the LORD surrounds his people") I am taken back in my mind to my school days and the view from my desert hills. For me as a child, mountains just *looked* secure and comforting. For ancient people, mountains surrounding a city actually provided a line of defense from invading enemies.

God is to his people a sure line of defense. He surrounds them completely and always. Those who trust in him, who know him as their God and are united to his Son, are themselves like a mountain. They are like a mountain, our key verse tells us, because they cannot be moved. Instead, they abide forever. Whatever happens, God remains their God and keeps them to be with him forever.

We've considered the permanence of mountains—but what if one *did* move? What if we saw familiar mountains suddenly uprooted and sliding into the sea? Wouldn't *that* be disturbing? One of the psalms describes such a scene as a metaphor for saying that even when the most upsetting, disturbing events occur in their lives, God's people can continue to trust him and have no need to be afraid. "God is our refuge and strength, a very present help in trouble. Therefore we will not fear though the earth gives way, though the mountains be moved into the heart of the sea" (Ps. 46:1–2).

A firm rock, an eternal dwelling, a mountain surrounding his people, a refuge, a help in trouble—all this God is to his people, but only to his people. Those who are not his people have no relationship with him, except as his enemies. To those who come to him through Christ, God is everything they will ever need and so much more.

As for me and my house . . .

- Is God your rock? Are you among the people of God who will dwell in him, generation after generation? Have you turned *from* whatever idols attract you, to God through faith in his Son? Do you know him as your ever present help in trouble?

God Owns the Land

Korah's Rebellion

Numbers 16

"Serve the Lord with fear,
and rejoice with trembling."

Psalm 2:11

Someone had to be in charge! You can't move hundreds of thousands of people from slavery in Egypt to a land far away without someone in charge. God had chosen Moses to be that someone.

Someone had to be the high priest. Sinners cannot come into the presence of a holy God without a mediator, someone to offer sacrifices on their behalf, making atonement with God for the sins that offend him. God had chosen Aaron to be that high priest.

Korah, Dathan, and Abiram didn't like God's choices. "Why do we need Aaron for a priest?" they complained. "We're all holy. And as for Moses—he brought us out of Egypt where we had plenty to eat into this horrible wilderness, and he's trying to make himself a prince among us. We don't want to do what he says anymore—and we're not going to!"

Korah, Dathan, and Abiram forgot something important. When we rebel against the leaders God has given us, we rebel against God. The three men began to talk to others about how they felt. First they convinced their own families that Moses and Aaron were not to be respected. Then they began to encourage others of God's people to rebel against their leaders. God is the Lord of all he has made, including people. He expects obedience from his creatures, and it angers him when they refuse to give it.

At God's command, Moses told the Israelites to get away from the tents of Korah, Dathan, and Abiram. "This is how you'll know God has sent me to lead this people," Moses announced. "If these men die a natural death like anyone else, then the Lord hasn't sent me. But if the Lord creates something new, and the ground opens its mouth and swallows them alive, with all they have, then you shall know that these men have despised not just me, but the Lord."

What a claim! As soon as Moses had made it, the Israelites watched in horror as it happened: the ground split apart under the tents that belonged to the rebels. The men, their families, and all that they had fell, still living, into the pit that opened under them. Then the earth closed back up again. How could such a thing happen? It could happen because, unlike Korah, Dathan, and Abiram, the ground recognizes its Lord and obeys it perfectly. If God commands the ground to do something it has never done, it will do it.

Many people say, as these rebels did, "We are all holy," and assume they can come to God as they are. They don't think they need a priest. They refuse to come to God in the only way he has given us—through his Son, the perfect high priest who offered the perfect sacrifice of his own blood. The Bible tells us that a pit will open for them one day and they'll be thrown into it, because their names are not found in the Lamb's book of life (Rev. 20:15).

Many people say about Jesus, as people in one of his parables said, "We do not want this man to reign over us" (Luke 19:14). Those who never bow the knee to Christ in this life will bow to him when he returns, but it will be too late. They will be cast away from God and from his people forever.

As for me and my house . . .

- Think through what it means to carry out both parts of the key verse at the same time.
- See the key verse in its context by reading Psalm 2, which describes God's attitude toward those who reject his chosen ruler.

18

Look at All the Food!

God's Goodness in the Foods We Eat

"You cause the grass to grow for the livestock
and plants for man to cultivate,
that he may bring forth food from the earth
and wine to gladden the heart of man,
oil to make his face shine
and bread to strengthen man's heart."

Psalm 104:14–15

O n the third day of creation, God did more than just gather all the land into continents and islands. He also covered that land with all kinds of plants. When we consider how essential plant life is for animals, fish, birds, and people, we see the wisdom and provision of God in creating it for us. Plants give off oxygen, which people and animals need. And of course, a plant of some kind is at the bottom of every food chain. In creating plant life, God provided for the needs of his creatures.

We see God's faithfulness in continuing to provide for his creatures when we consider how he keeps plants growing. People can plant seeds and fertilize and water them, but ultimately God must cause a plant to grow. The psalmist wrote: "You visit the earth and water it; you greatly enrich it; . . . you provide their grain, for so you have prepared it. You water its furrows abundantly, settling its ridges, softening it with showers, and blessing its growth" (Ps. 65:9–10).

Have you ever stopped to consider that God could have made just one food that provided all the nutrition we needed? Think of a food that comes from a plant that you really don't like. What if that were the only kind of food there was? It would give you all the vitamins, minerals, and proteins you'd need, but every time you ate it, you would feel like gagging. Or God could have created tasteless pills that grew on trees. Once a day, we would swallow them and have all our needs met. No gagging that way, but where's the fun in swallowing a pill?

When we see the great variety of foods that grow on plants, we see the great goodness of God. He didn't content himself merely with providing for people's nutritional needs; he created many different things for us to enjoy. If there are a few foods we don't like, we can live our entire lives never having to eat them and still have plenty of other things to nourish our bodies. Consider the sweetness of sugar, the juiciness of an orange, the crispness of celery, the earthiness of freshly-baked bread, the joy of chocolate. These are only a few of the good gifts God created when he created the plant world.

Not only the food that comes from plants but the plants themselves are demonstrations of God's goodness and of his love for beauty. Do you realize how many different kinds of palm trees alone there are? Trees provide beauty, homes for the birds with their happy songs, and shade when it's hot. Flowers not only delight our eyes, they fill the earth with fragrances of all kinds. We wouldn't really need different foods, beautiful trees, or colorful, sweet-smelling flowers. They are the overflow of God's goodness to us. "Every good gift and every perfect gift is from above, coming down from the Father of lights. . . ." (James 1:17).

As for me and my house . . .

- See how long a list you can make with your family of foods that come from plants.

- Work through the alphabet trying to think of a different kind of plant for each letter. Thank God for his faithfulness in feeding his creatures and for his goodness in making so many plants just to give us pleasure.

All Dressed Up

God's Provision Seen in the Flowers

"And why are you anxious about clothing? Consider the lilies of the field, how they grow: they neither toil nor spin, yet I tell you, even Solomon in all his glory was not arrayed like one of these. But if God so clothes the grass of the field, which today is alive and tomorrow is thrown into the oven, will he not much more clothe you, O you of little faith?"

Matthew 6:28–30

Hot pink, deep purple, or red-and-white candy-striped tulips; roses, with their variety of colors *and* their different smells; bright yellow daffodils; happy little daisies; giant sunflowers; clean-smelling lavender—these are only a few of the many flowers that fill our earth with beauty and fragrance. Gardeners grow some flowers on purpose, experimenting and working to develop new varieties. Other flowers grow wild, on prairies and meadows, or in forests and jungles.

Flowers have one drawback: they never last long. They bud, blossom, open to full size, then close and shrivel, all in no more than a few days—sometimes in only a few hours. If we made flowers, would we spend so much time making billions of lovely things that would die so quickly? Flowers show, again, God's overflowing goodness and generosity. He has lavished so much careful design and such artistry on them, knowing his creatures would enjoy them.

Jesus used the beauty of flowers to demonstrate why his people never need to worry that their physical needs will go unmet. He asked his disciples, how much is grass worth? Grass is common, growing everywhere on its own. Yet God has "arrayed" it—dressed it up, decorated it—with a multitude of gorgeous flowers. Not even King Solomon, the wealthiest man of his day, could dress to compete with the "clothing" God has put on common grass. God values his people so much more than he values grass; will he not, surely, provide what they need to wear? Jesus went on to say that since God's people have a heavenly Father who can do anything, and since he knows exactly what they need, they never have to be anxious about what they need. They're free, instead, to spend their energy growing to be like Jesus and helping his kingdom to grow.

One place you would never expect to see the beauty of flowers is in the desert. So little rain falls in a desert and, in many deserts, the heat is so brutal that frail little flowers could never survive. Deserts specialize in plants that poke and prick, like the many kinds of cacti God created. Yet even cactus plants produce beautiful blossoms—some fragrant, some in brilliant colors— for a short time in the spring. And even the harsh desert, after an unusually rainy winter, will appear all decked out in spring finery with flowers covering the ground and filling the bushes. Before God sent his Son, prophets spoke of deserts bursting into bloom as a metaphor for the beauty and glory of salvation that the Savior would bring. Sin-wasted hearts, ugly and dead before, would flower and bear beautiful fruit for the glory of God. "For the LORD comforts Zion; he comforts all her waste places and makes her wilderness like Eden, her desert like the garden of the LORD . . ." (Isa. 51:3).

As for me and my house . . .

- Take a walk or visit a garden or a nursery. Count the number of different kinds of flowers you see. Look closely at several of them, paying special attention to their smell, color, and design. Praise our beautiful God for creating such beauty, for providing for the needs of his people, and for turning their desert-like hearts into gardens.

20

God Owns the Plants

Aaron's Rod Blossoms

Numbers 17

"And there is salvation in no one else, for there is no other name under heaven given among men by which we must be saved."

Acts 4:12

Y ou would think that the Israelites would have learned their lesson. They had watched, horrified, as the ground had opened under the tents of the men who had spoken against Moses and Aaron. They had watched as fire fell from heaven and consumed men who had offered incense when God had not appointed them to do so. They had heard how God had commanded that a covering for the altar be made of the gold from the dead men's censers. This covering, God had said, would "be a reminder to the people of Israel, so that no outsider, who is not of the descendants of Aaron, should draw near to burn incense before the LORD" (Num. 16:40), and become like the rebels who had lost their lives.

You wouldn't think that *the very next day* these Israelites would be grumbling against Moses and Aaron again, but that's just what happened. The Israelites complained that it was Moses and Aaron who had killed these rebels among God's people.

God responded in wrath. "Get away from these people," he told Moses and Aaron, "because I'm going to destroy them all instantly." Infuriating as these people could be, Moses and Aaron did not want them destroyed. What could they do to turn away God's wrath?

Moses understood that God had appointed Aaron as the high priest. He understood that this was precisely because people sin and bring down

God's wrath every day. They must have a mediator to make atonement for them, and Aaron was the one God had chosen. So Moses told Aaron to take his censer with fire and incense from God's altar and to carry it to the congregation to make atonement for them. A plague had already begun, and already 14,700 people had died from it. But Aaron made atonement, as he had been appointed to do, and the plague stopped.

That made it clear who was the true high priest. That showed who had the God-given ability to offer sacrifices for sin that would turn away God's anger. But to make sure the Israelites really got the point, God told Moses to collect staffs, one from a leader of each of the twelve tribes, and Aaron's staff as well. "Put all the staffs in the tent of meeting, where I meet with you," God told him. "The staff of the man whom I have chosen as high priest will have budded by morning."

A staff is like a wooden broomstick. It's a piece of dead wood. It doesn't grow anything. But because plants belong to God and obey him, Aaron's staff had indeed budded in the morning. Not only had buds grown on it, but full blossoms and fruit—ripe almonds—as well.

God alone establishes the rules for how we come to him. The Israelites could only come into God's presence by means of God's appointed priest offering sacrifices for them. This was a picture of Christ, the only mediator between God and man, and the one alone whom God has appointed to save us from our sin.

As for me and my house . . .

- The words of our key verse are just as true as they were when Peter said them two thousand years ago. Pray for boldness to point people to Christ as the only way to God, even though people have become increasingly hostile to this idea. Pray for those you know who have not yet come to God through Christ.

Like the Grass

Short Lives and Lasting Realities

"All flesh is grass,
and all its beauty is like the flower of the field.
The grass withers, the flower fades
when the breath of the LORD blows on it;
surely the people are grass.
The grass withers, the flower fades,
but the word of our God will stand forever."

Isaiah 40:6–8

Human beings and flowers have two things in common. If you take the time to stop and really look at a flower, you will be amazed at its beauty and design. It is a thing of glory! When you stop and consider the design of a human being in all his or her parts, you will also be amazed. They are also glorious! Children grow and develop, learning a tremendous amount of information and abilities in their first few years. Young men are handsome and strong; young women are beautiful. Humans are intelligent and creative; we marvel at all they can understand, make, and invent.

Yet, for all their beauty, flowers have very short lives. Today they stop us in our tracks with their brilliance; tomorrow they are withered and gone. Humans too, for all the glory of what we are and what we can do, really don't live long. Time might seem to pass slowly when you're young, but the older you get, the faster life seems to go by. The bent-over, gray-haired man shuffling down the road was a strong young Marine or a star high school quarterback only a few years ago. The lady who shakes all over and has to use a walker was an energetic young mom not long ago, and before that, a beautiful girl in a prom dress.

It's sad to see people you love grow old and lose the good looks and the energy and maybe even the sharp mind they once had. It's frightening when it happens to you. Most people try to not think about growing old and dying, and they try not to notice it happening to those they love. But if we and those we love know God as our God, we can accept the changes time brings to our bodies, because those things which are most important will endure even after time has ended.

Our key verse tells us that the word of our God will stand forever. The things he has told us are true will always be true. The promises he has made will always endure. God will continue to keep those promises even when some of his people become too old to remember them.

Psalm 103 also reminds us of how much people are like grass and flowers—quick to flourish, quick to disappear—and it contrasts our short lives with God's covenant love. To those who are in God's covenant through Christ, his love remains always the same. It is "from everlasting to everlasting on those who fear him" (v. 17). God doesn't change in any way; we can take comfort in that, for we long for permanence even in the midst of all our changes. God's righteous character will continue righteous, generation after generation.

The Bible is full of warnings on the folly of giving ourselves to the pursuit of things that don't last. It calls us to seek God and his kingdom, to know and obey his Word, because these will endure forever. Doesn't that just make sense?

As for me and my house . . .

- Read the parable in Luke 12:13–21 where Jesus illustrates the folly of investing in things that seem all-important to most of us, but that really have no lasting value.

- List some things people could spend time on that will have value for only a little while, if at all. List things people could invest their time in that will go on having value into eternity.

Look at All the Fruit!

Jesus Is the True Vine

*"I am the vine; you are the branches. Whoever abides in me and I in him,
he it is that bears much fruit, for apart from me you can do nothing."*

John 15:5

Perhaps, looking for a way to communicate to his people what their relationship with him would be like, Jesus looked around himself, there in ancient Israel, and noticed all the vineyards filled with grapevines. Aha! he thought. That's what it's like. Perhaps. But I think that, instead, before there were any grapevines or any people at all, God created grapevines with the specific idea of making something his people could see that would help them understand how they would be related to the Savior he would send.

Back in Old Testament times, before Jesus came, God became angry when his people had taken all his gifts and all the advantages he had given them, and then had failed to live for him as he intended them to do. The prophet Isaiah compared God to a farmer and Israel to a vineyard. God had planted the vineyard in the best possible place. He had provided everything it would need to be a fruitful vineyard. Yet it produced no good grapes at all, only wild ones. "What more was there to do for my vineyard, that I have not done in it?" Isaiah wrote, on God's behalf. "He looked for justice," Isaiah continued, speaking of God, "but behold, bloodshed; for righteousness, but behold, an outcry!" (Isa. 5:4, 7).

Israel could not produce good grapes. The nation was made up of sinners who could not stop sinning—nor did they want to. Because of their sin, God's Old Testament people were not capable of producing fruit for the glory of God.

Jesus came, announcing, "I am the true vine." Being sinless, he could do those things that were pleasing to God. Jesus explained how his followers could bear fruit for God's glory. He himself is the vine,; his people are the branches. Grapes naturally grow on the branches of a grapevine, as long as the branch is part of the vine. The grapevine itself does everything necessary to grow the grapes. It soaks up the sun. Its roots draw up water and nourishment from the soil. The sap in the grapevine's trunk flows to all the branches and, in the right season, the grapes appear. The branch produces those grapes just by being connected to the vine.

If a branch is broken off, of course, it dies. A branch cut off from the vine will never grow a single grape. Even though we can't see it with our physical eyes, the connection God's people have with the Lord Jesus Christ is as close and as important as the connection a branch has to a vine. God's people abide in Jesus. We cling to Jesus in faith, depend on and trust Jesus for all we need, and follow Jesus' commands. Jesus abides in us by the Holy Spirit he has given to live in us. Apart from our vine, we would be just like the Israelites of Isaiah's day, unable to produce any fruit pleasing to God. Abiding in Jesus, the true vine, we bear much fruit for the glory of God.

As for me and my house . . .

- Read the entire vineyard passage in Isaiah 5:1–7, then the entire "I am the true vine" passage in John 15:1–11.

- See if you can find something bearing fruit near your home— perhaps a grapevine or a fruit tree or a tomato plant. Observe the different parts of the plant and contrast the live, fruitful branches with any dead ones you see on the ground. Thank God for sending the true vine, so we could bear fruit for him as we were created to do.

Day 4

Sun, Moon, and Stars

To Infinity and Beyond!

Outer Space and a God with No Limits

"The heavens declare the glory of God,
and the sky above proclaims his handiwork."

Psalm 19:1

O n the fourth day of the creation week, God created lights to separate night from day, to mark off seasons and years, and to give light upon the earth (Gen. 1:14–15). We call those lights the sun, the moon, and the stars. Ever since their creation, they have faithfully traveled through the paths God ordained for them. And they have filled humans with wonder at their beauty.

Of all created things, outer space is what makes most of us feel the smallest. To be somewhere out of the city on a clear night and step outside and look up at the stars is to feel tiny and insignificant in such a vast universe.

Job spoke of God and of the things God has done that are such mysteries to us. Job said, "He stretches out the north over the void and hangs the earth on nothing. . . . He has inscribed a circle on the face of the waters at the boundary between light and darkness" (Job 26:7, 10). But then Job went on to add, "Behold, these are but the outskirts of his ways . . ." (Job 26:14). Even something so great and amazing as the mysteries of outer space are just the very outer edges of what God can do. The things that most astound us about creation are almost nothing compared to the richness and fullness of who God is. Job added, "How small a whisper do we hear of him!" Creation reveals to us true things about God, but those things show so little of all there is to know that it turns out to be just the barest little whisper about him. If we look at creation and say, "Wow. That's awesome. Now I know what God is like," and stop there, we've missed it. God is so much greater and grander and more majestic than the most wonderful things he has made.

More than anything else we can look at, the night sky gives us a sense of the infinite. The word infinite means having no limits. Everything we see around us has limits. We have limits. There are limits to what we can do. We have limits of space; we can only be in one place at a time. There are limits to how long we live. There was a time when our lives began (that's a limit on one end of life for us) and there will be a time when we will die (a limit on the other end of life). God alone is infinite, having no limits at all. There is nothing he wants to do that he cannot do. He fills all places at the same time.

The night sky and outer space remind us of the greatness and vastness of our God. We don't know where the universe ends. No one has discovered the end of it. For all practical purposes, as far as human beings are concerned, it goes on and on forever. It *appears* infinite. God, the Creator of it all, truly is infinite. He has no beginning and no end. No one will ever find out all there is to know about God because everything about him is without limit.

As for me and my house . . .

- Plan a time with no moon (or just a small one) and a place with no man-made light when you can spend time looking at the night sky. Praise God that he is great—even greater than the entire universe, his creation—and that he has no limits at all.

He Guides the Stars by Name

The Omniscience and Omnipotence of God

"He determines the number of the stars;
he gives to all of them their names.
Great is our Lord, and abundant in power;
his understanding is beyond measure."

Psalm 147:4–5

Camping on a clear night, you can look up and see countless pinpricks of light as well as what looks like a long strand of wispy cloud. The cloudy, or milky, looking thing is what we can see from earth of the Milky Way, the galaxy containing our sun, our earth, and all our planets. What looks like cloud or haze is really many, many stars so far away that we cannot see them clearly. Their combined light gives the effect of a bright cloud.

The Milky Way contains billions of stars. One estimate is between two hundred billion and four hundred billion stars. And the Milky Way is only one of billions of galaxies in the universe, each galaxy with hundreds of billions of stars of its own. That's a lot of stars! As you can see, those numbers are not very precise, and they're only astronomers' best guesses. No one knows for sure, especially since there is only so much of the universe that can be observed from earth.

God knows the exact number of the stars. Our key verse says he not only knows it, he determined it. He decided exactly how many stars there would be. Like the stars, our key verse tells us, God's understanding is beyond measure. The best scientists have limits to what they know. Like everything else about him, God's knowledge is infinite. We use the word omniscient to speak of God. *Omni* means "all" and *scient* means "knowing." God is *omniscient*—knowing all.

Some of the stars in the Milky Way are grouped together in what astronomers call "globular clusters." Each globular cluster holds anywhere from tens of thousands to millions of stars. Imagine trying to name all the stars in a globular cluster! That would be impossible, so scientists just name the clusters, not all the individual stars. They give the clusters uncreative names like "M4" or "M13." Our key verse also tells us that not only does God know how many stars there are, he has *names* for all of them!

"Lift up your eyes on high and see," the prophet Isaiah said about the stars. "Who created these? He who brings out their host by number, calling them all by name, by the greatness of his might, and because he is strong in power not one of them is missing" (Isa. 40:26). Another *omni* word we use when describing God is *omnipotence*. Again, *omni* means "all." *Potent* means "having power." To say that God is *omnipotent* is to say that he has all power.

God in his omniscience knows the numbers and the names of the stars. God's omnipotence preserves the stars. Once, God asked Job: "Can you bind the chains of the Pleiades or loose the cords of Orion? Can you lead forth the Mazzaroth [evidently the ancient name for a constellation] in their season, or can you guide the Bear with its children?" (Job 38:31–32). God has bound the constellations to regular paths. He guides them because he has decreed when and where they will appear and how they will move across the sky. "Do you know the ordinances of the heavens?" God went on to ask Job. "Can you establish their rule on the earth?" The heavens obey God's ordinances. They are so sure and so fixed that, for centuries before modern technology, sailors and other travelers used the stars in the night sky to figure out where they were and how to get to where they wanted to go. The stars declare the omniscience and the omnipotence of our God.

As for me and my house . . .

- Going outside several times in one night or using a planetarium, observe the movement of one or more constellations across the sky. Praise God for faithfully guiding them every night.

- What else does God know because of his omniscience? What else can he do because of his omnipotence? (And just answering "everything" is cheating!)

Nothing Hidden from Its Heat

The Sun and the Omnipresence of God

"In them he has set a tent for the sun. . . .
Its rising is from the end of the heavens,
and its circuit to the end of them,
and there is nothing hidden from its heat."

Psalm 19:4, 6

On the fourth day of creation, God created our sun. One might say it's just another star, one among billions, not particularly significant. It is, however, very important to us! God said to Job, "Have you commanded the morning since your days began . . . ?" (Job 38:12). Why does the sun rise every morning? Because God has commanded that it should. Jesus said God causes his sun to rise upon the evil and the good. The fact that day always dawns is a loud and clear statement that God rules and that he is good to his creatures. How well would we get along without the sun? What would happen if sometimes the sun came up and sometimes it didn't and you never knew for sure when it would? God is a God of order and faithfulness. Even people who deny God get up every morning enjoying the security of a regular sunrise.

Of course, our sun gives off far more heat than any of us ever feel. We see God's wisdom and design in the atmosphere that surrounds our earth. If it weren't there to protect us, we would be instantly burned alive. The moon has no atmosphere. In the daytime, its surface gets so hot that if it had any rivers, they would boil. At night, the moon is so cold that any rivers would freeze. Can it really be just by chance that the planet we live on is the only one known so far that has exactly the conditions we need to live?

When David wrote in the nineteenth psalm that the heavens declare the glory of God, he also said that "their voice goes out through all the earth, and their words to the end of the world . . ." (Ps. 19:4). As a shepherd and then as a soldier, David had slept outside many times. He realized that no matter where he was when he looked up at night, he saw the same stars. When he rose in the morning, the sun was always either already up or it would be up soon. Sometimes it might be hidden behind clouds, but no matter where he traveled, David always found the sun to be there too. In his psalm, David pointed out that everywhere on earth, people could see God's glory in the skies. He said that the sun travels from one end of the earth to the other and nothing is hidden from its heat.

If nothing on earth can hide from the sun, how much more is that true of the sun's creator, God? "Can a man hide himself in secret places so that I cannot see him? declares the LORD. Do I not fill heaven and earth? declares the LORD" (Jer. 23:24). In another psalm, David celebrated the fact that God would be with him anywhere, even if he could go deep into the sea or under the ground (Ps. 139:7–12). While the sun's light touches every spot on the face of the planet, God alone is truly omnipresent—in all places at the same time. Like many of God's creatures, the sun can, in some small way, picture something about God. Still, God is separate from and greater than the sun and all creation.

As for me and my house . . .

- When might it be uncomfortable to realize that God is in all places at all times? When might it be very comforting to know God is omnipresent?

- When you get up tomorrow, check to see if the sun came up (even though it might be behind a cloud). Praise God for his good and faithful provision.

God Owns the Sun, Moon, and Stars

Joshua's Victory over Canaanite Kings

Joshua 10:1–15

"Yours is the day, yours also the night;
*   you have established the heavenly lights and the sun."*

Psalm 74:16

We are so used to what goes on in the sky that we take it for granted. Every morning the sun rises; every evening it sets. Every night stars are out, even if sometimes we can't see them because of clouds or pollution. Every month the moon goes through the same cycle: first a little fingernail, then a quarter, a half, three-quarters, and finally a full moon. It's all as regular as clockwork! It is so regular that we actually set our clocks and make our calendars based on what happens in the sky. Because it's so consistent, we sometimes forget that it is God who controls it all. He ordained that the sun, moon, and stars follow their same patterns, and they obey, day after day and year after year. The countless stars and the vast reaches of outer space obey their creator, God.

There was once a day when the sun did not set at its appointed time, and the moon and stars failed to come out on schedule. But that was not because they suddenly disobeyed God; rather, it was in obedience to God who owns them and who can do with them whatever he chooses.

The Israelites had just entered Canaan, the land God had promised to give them. God had promised to enable them to drive out the people who already lived there, and he had commanded them to destroy those people completely because of the centuries of their wickedness and idolatry. Some of the Canaanites knew what was coming and feared the Israelites and their

God. Some of these people devised a trick and deceived the Israelites into thinking they were from some other land, when really they lived in Gibeon in Canaan. These Gibeonites fooled Joshua and the leaders into making a covenant with them. The Gibeonites would serve the Israelites, and the Israelites would never fight against them but would protect them. Even after the Israelites discovered the trick, they honored their covenant with the people of Gibeon.

Five kings of other cities in Canaan heard about the peace Gibeon had made with the Israelites. "The traitors!" they said, and they banded together to attack Gibeon and punish them. The Gibeonites sent a message to Joshua, pleading for help. God promised Joshua that he and the Israelites would win this battle. The Israelites marched all night and launched a sneak attack. God threw the soldiers of the five kings into a panic, and they fled before Joshua and his men. God also threw down giant hailstones on the fleeing army, killing many.

All day the Israelites fought the Canaanite armies, but finally the end of the day drew near. The battle was not finished, for God had commanded Joshua to kill them all. If darkness fell, the enemy soldiers would be able to escape under its cover. Joshua prayed and then commanded the sun and the moon to stand still. They remained right where they were until Joshua and the Israelites had completed the task God had given them. The Bible says, "There has been no day like it before or since, when the LORD heeded the voice of a man, for the LORD fought for Israel" (Josh. 10:14).

As for me and my house . . .

- "The Lord heeded the voice of a man" because that man was seeking to faithfully obey what God had commanded him to do. The Lord still fights on behalf of his people—but only his people, those who are faithfully seeking to obey him. Look in John 6:29 and Acts 2:38 to discover the very first commandments any person must obey.

Sunrise from on High and Bright Morning Star

Our Lord and Savior

"And we have something more sure, the prophetic word, to which you will do well to pay attention as to a lamp shining in a dark place, until the day dawns and the morning star rises in your hearts."

2 Peter 1:19

Have you ever gone camping and not been able to sleep? You lie there in your sleeping bag, unable to get comfortable. Maybe you're cold, or maybe you're lying on a hard spot, or maybe your sleeping bag is hopelessly tangled up. The longer you lie there, the more uncomfortable you get, and, at last, you decide you will not sleep this whole night and you just wish morning would come. It's lonely and boring just lying there while everyone else sleeps. When the sky finally begins to lighten, you're glad. Soon the sun will rise and you'll get up, leaving the miserable night behind.

People who have to stay awake through the night greet the rising sun even more gladly. Perhaps someone has a night job or has guard duty or must stay by the bed of someone who's sick. When the sun finally rises, someone else will come take that person's place so the one who stayed up all night can rest.

Can you imagine a night that never ends? What if the sun never rose and the darkness just went on forever? That would be a good description of the sinful human heart if Jesus had never come. In the Old Testament, Isaiah promised that people who walked in darkness would see a great light. He said the Lord would rise on his people (Isa. 9:2; 60:2–3).

Zechariah may have been the first to realize that this prophecy came true in the Lord Jesus Christ. Zechariah, the childless old man, saw an angel in the temple. The angel promised him a child who would prepare the way for the Lord. When the child was born, Zechariah sang a song praising God for keeping his promises and sending a Savior. In his song, he said his little son, John, would grow up to give God's people the knowledge of salvation through the forgiveness of their sin. Zechariah said that, because of God's tender mercy, the sunrise from on high would come. He would "give light to those who sit in darkness and in the shadow of death . . ." (Luke 1:79).

Jesus came like the sun, bursting in on the hopelessness of sin and death that had ruled up until then. No sunrise ever made so drastic a contrast with the night that had gone before!

He will come again, and those who watch for him long to see him the way a watchman waits to see the morning star, the one that rises just before dawn and promises that the darkness is almost past and a new day is just around the corner.

A glorious eternal day is about to dawn. The morning star is about to rise. Jesus will return soon. What do we do while we wait? Peter wrote that we're to pay attention to "the prophetic word," to Scripture, as to a lamp shining in a dark place. It will provide all the light we need until he comes. We must come to know it well and rely on it while we wait for the day.

As for me and my house . . .

- Read Zechariah's whole song in Luke 1:67–79 and rejoice with him at the light and joy Jesus brought with the salvation he accomplished.

- Get up before dawn one morning. Use a flashlight to find your way outside, then see if you see a morning star (usually the planet Venus). Consider how important a light is while it's dark. Is Scripture that important to you?

Day 5

Birds and Fish

In Wisdom Have You Made Them All
Birds and God's Wisdom

"O Lᴏʀᴅ, how manifold are your works!
  In wisdom have you made them all;
  the earth is full of your creatures."

Psalm 104:24

Give yourself a minute and see how many different kinds of birds you can think of in that much time. You can probably name quite a few, but do you realize that experts estimate the number of different bird species to be around ten thousand? All those different species have different habits, different food needs, and different kinds of homes. That's why they all look so different from each other. God designed each kind of bird so it can do just what it needs to do to be able to survive on its food and in its habitat.

Compare the roadrunner of North, South, and Central America with the emperor penguin of the Antarctic. Neither bird does much flying, but that's one of the only things they have in common. The roadrunner eats lizards, snakes, and small animals, which it can catch due to its running speed. A roadrunner will enjoy a rattlesnake dinner after catching a snake, tossing it in the air, and biting it in two on its way down. Penguins dine on small fish and animals they catch deep underwater. They store far more oxygen in their bodies than other creatures do, drawing on it when they dive after their meals and slowing their hearts to five beats a minute to use less of it. If the roadrunner went to visit the emperor penguin, he would never survive. The roadrunner is used to hot desert temperatures, even over 120 degrees, while the penguin lives in temperatures as low as 80 degrees below zero. When "God created . . . every winged bird according to its kind," he gave the roadrunner and the penguin both the necessary equipment to live and thrive in their extreme weather conditions.

Some bird species move, or migrate, every year in order to have suitable temperatures and adequate food. When God said, "Let birds fly above the earth across the expanse of the heavens," he not only made them able to fly—an amazing enough feat—but he built into many birds the ability to fly incredible distances without getting lost. Seabirds travel the farthest, because they can fly over oceans and still rest on the water and find food to eat. The Arctic Tern has the longest flight, traveling from the Arctic to the Antarctic—the length of our whole planet! Other migratory birds, not made to rest and eat out on the ocean, have to fly from one land area to another. Some of these birds store enough body fat to fly for a long time over water without landing. The Bar-tailed Godwit has the longest nonstop flight of any bird, flying all the way from Alaska to New Zealand without ever stopping— a flight of seven thousand miles. Other birds cannot fly very long at all, so God made them to rely on air currents on which they can glide. The migrations of these birds must be over land and during the daytime to catch the rising warm air they need.

Our planet boasts a tremendous variety of habitats: oceans, jungles, mountains, deserts, frozen wastelands, and prairies. Each area has its own bird species, and each species was designed in wisdom, with painstaking attention to detail, by our infinitely wise God.

As for me and my house . . .

- As you study any form of life, notice the careful design of each creature that you study. Don't allow anyone to tell you that these things just evolved. With birds alone, there are ten thousand different, complex designs! Could enough time ever pass for all those bird designs to just happen by chance?

Wonderful Are Your Works!

God's Wisdom Seen in the Fish

"Let heaven and earth praise him,
the seas and everything that moves in them."

Psalm 69:34

O n the same creation day that God said, "Let birds fly above the earth," he also said, "Let the waters swarm with swarms of living creatures." And, of course, it was so. Centuries later, a psalmist wrote, "Here is the sea, great and wide, which teems with creatures innumerable, living things both small and great" (Ps. 104:25). So far, scientists are aware of twenty-five thousand different kinds of fish, and they discover many new species every year! And that's just the fish. All kinds of creatures—oysters, shrimp, lobsters, whales—that *aren't* fish swarm in the waters of our planet as well. In the same way that we marvel at God's mighty acts of creation when we consider all the different kinds of birds, so too we will marvel when we consider the many creatures that live in the water.

There's great diversity among winged creatures. A hummingbird is quite different from an ostrich. A peacock is larger and far more beautiful than a sparrow. The variety among water creatures, though, is even greater. An eel looks nothing like starfish and a crab has very little in common with a dolphin. Among birds, we compared emperor penguins in their frozen homeland to roadrunners in their hot deserts. Fish also live in both extremes. Antarctic ice fish can live in waters so cold they would freeze the blood of other living creatures, while desert pupfish survive in waters that are over 100 degrees. God filled the waters of our entire planet with creatures, creating thousands of different kinds, each uniquely designed to live in its particular habitat, eating its particular diet.

Starfish, for example, come in many sizes and many colors and live in many different areas. One thing they all have in common is their design, ideal for eating creatures that live in shells. The starfish's arms are covered with suction cups. When they latch onto the two halves of a shell with their arms, those suction cups steadily suck, exerting a constant pull that finally pries the shell open. What's even more amazing is that the starfish is designed so that he can push his own stomach to the outside of his body to digest the creature he found between the shell halves. When he's finished, he pulls his stomach back inside.

Sharks have ideal equipment for finding their food. For one thing, their sense of smell is so sharp that they can pick up the scent of a few drops of something (blood, for instance) even when it's mixed into great quantities of water (like the ocean!). And they can pick up that scent from far, far away. To enable sharks to sneak up on what they want to eat, God made them dark on the top and light on the underside. A fish looking up from the ocean floor sees light close to the surface; looking down into the ocean depths, a creature sees darkness. The shark is colored so that he mixes in with the light and shadow. His streamlined body makes him capable of short bursts of speed to catch his prey. His mouth is on the underside of his body so he can scoop up dead or dying things on the ocean floor.

As for me and my house . . .

- Plan a trip to an aquarium where you can marvel at God's manifold and wonderful works.

- Praise God for his amazing, detailed, precise designs, unique for each creature's needs.

God Owns the Birds

Ravens Feed Elijah

1 Kings 17:1–7

"Is it by your understanding that the hawk soars
    and spreads his wings toward the south?
Is it at your command that the eagle mounts up
    and makes his nest on high?"

Job 39:26–27

E lijah looked the king right in the eye. Now was the moment to say what he had come to say. He knew King Ahab would not like this news, but it was why God had sent him, and declare it he must.

"As the LORD, the God of Israel, lives, before whom I stand, there shall be neither dew nor rain these years, except by my word," Elijah announced solemnly.

Elijah could see Ahab's reaction all over his face. *Does this nobody think he's stronger than Baal? Baal is the one who sends rain. This man can't prevent it! And how dare he speak to me like this! I'm the king!*

God, watching over his courageous prophet, told him to leave that place and go to the brook Cherith, where he should hide. God had a plan to prove to his sinning people that *he* was God, not Baal. *He* was the one who sent—or withheld—rain. God's plan would take a while though. First, he had to show that, if he withheld rain, no one else could provide it. He would bring the Israelites to a point of desperation by allowing no moisture to fall. Then, his prophet Elijah would challenge the prophets of Baal—Queen Jezebel's idol, who supposedly caused rain and storms—to a contest. Whoever could make it rain as an answer to prayer would be the true God.

But for now, Elijah must wait for the years with no rain to pass. But what would he do about food and water? If there were no rain for crops and no food for the people, what would Elijah eat? When God told Elijah to hide by the brook Cherith, he told him he could drink water from the brook. As for food, "I have commanded the ravens to feed you," God told him.

Ravens? Ravens are scavengers. They eat anything they find. They're not like squirrels, which carry their food off and store it somewhere for later. A hungry raven goes out looking for food and eats what he finds as soon as he finds it. That's how God made them.

Nor are ravens tame birds. They don't share what they have. *This should be interesting*, Eljiah may have thought, but off he went to the brook, trusting God to do what he said he would do.

When the first mealtime came, Elijah saw a black speck far off in the distant sky. Then he saw another and another. Soon there were many black specks flying closer and closer and growing larger as they came. At last Elijah could see that they were all large, black birds and each one carried something in its beak. The first bird flew over Elijah, dropped what it was carrying, and flew away. The second bird did the same. So did the third. And on it went, until Elijah had all the food he needed.

Every morning and every evening, God sent the ravens, as long as Elijah lived there by the brook. The ravens belonged to God. He had made them. They did what he commanded—even though it wasn't what they would normally do.

As for me and my house . . .

- How will knowing that God commands every creature in his world free us from fearing accidents or disasters?

- How will knowing that God owns and commands all creatures free us to use our time to seek him and his will, instead of using it to gather large amounts of money and possessions?

God Owns the Fish

A Great Catch for Breakfast

John 21:1–14

*"Praise the L*ORD *from the earth,*
*   you great sea creatures and all deeps,*
fire and hail, snow and mist,
*   stormy wind fulfilling his word!"*

Psalm 148:7–8

There's nothing like a night out on the lake fishing to make you forget your troubles. Cool night air, bright stars overhead, splish-splashing waves, and the gentle rocking of the boat, with nothing to do but wait for fish. After all they'd been through in the last few weeks, Peter's suggestion to go fishing seemed like a great idea to John. They had seen miracles, had watched Jesus ride into Jerusalem applauded as a king, and had felt tensions between him and the Jewish leaders increase. They had witnessed Jesus' late night arrest and the horrors of his crucifixion. Just when life had been at its darkest, though, Jesus had risen from the dead, and they had all seen him alive. Too much for the mind to grasp! A night at their old work of catching fish would soothe their overwhelmed emotions.

So seven of Jesus' disciples got a boat and took it out onto the Sea of Galilee as darkness fell. They fished all night, though with no success. *Have we lost our touch?* John may have wondered. Now day was breaking and it was time to give up and go home.

"Hey!" a voice called across the water. The fishermen looked and could just make out a man standing on the shore. "Do you have any fish?" the man called.

John cupped his hands around his mouth, so his voice would carry over the splashing of the waves, and called back, "Nothing!"

The voice came across the lake again. "Cast the net on the right side of the boat, and you'll find some." There had been a time when John would have laughed at the very idea. How long had he and his brother James and their partners, Peter and Andrew, been fishing? Only all their lives. If there were any fish anywhere near, they would surely have found them after a whole night fishing. Once, though, about three years ago, something similar had happened. After John and his partners had fished an entire night and caught nothing, Jesus had asked to use a boat to teach from. When he had finished teaching, Jesus—a carpenter, not a fisherman—had told them to put out into deep water and let down their nets for a catch. They had done it, and had ended up with so many fish in the boat that the boat had begun to sink.

Now, on this early morning, when John and the other disciples let down their nets, they trapped so many fish they couldn't haul in the net. John knew for sure. "It's the Lord!" he said, and Peter, who had probably been thinking the same thing, jumped into the water, too impatient to wait for the boat to make its way to shore. John and the others followed, dragging the overflowing net behind them. When they got to shore, they found Jesus, Lord of heaven and earth, tending a charcoal fire and preparing their breakfast. Together the disciples enjoyed their third visit with the risen Jesus.

As for me and my house . . .

• Jesus performed many signs to demonstrate that he is the Son of God and the Lord of heaven and earth. We have stories in the gospels of him commanding disease, demons, winds and waves, death, and—several times—fish. Praise him for being God and for supplying plenty of evidence to show us that he is.

32

Not a Sparrow Falls

The Providence of God

"Are not two sparrows sold for a penny? And not one of them will fall to the ground apart from your Father. But even the hairs of your head are all numbered. Fear not, therefore; you are of more value than many sparrows."

Matthew 10:29–31

How would you like to hammer your nose against a tree every time you need to eat? A woodpecker eats the bugs that live inside tree trunks. The only drill he has, for making holes to get to them, is his nose (or beak), so he must hammer away at the tree trunk for his food if he wants to eat. The woodpecker doesn't mind this the way you would mind it! God has made the woodpecker's beak of extremely hard material, given him a powerful neck with which to hammer, and designed for him a long, sticky tongue for catching the bugs through the holes he makes.

In the same sermon where Jesus told his followers not to worry about their clothing since God dresses even the flowers so beautifully, Jesus also told them not to worry about what they would eat. "Look at the birds of the air," he said, "they neither sow nor reap nor gather into barns, and yet your heavenly Father feeds them. Are you not of more value than they?" (Matt. 6:26).

God provides not only the food the birds need, but also the equipment they need for getting that food. God causes flowers to produce nectar for hummingbirds. While a hummingbird is one of the smallest of birds, it's still too large to land on a flower and crawl into it after the nectar, like a bee does. So God gave the hummingbird the ability to hover in the air in one spot, like a helicopter. As the tiny bird hovers, he pokes his long, narrow beak (also designed by God) into the flower and sucks out the nectar he needs.

The Bible tells us that God provides the food and even the breath all his creatures need, even the most insignificant of them. It also tells us that when anything happens to any of God's creatures—again, even the most insignificant—God is involved. The example Jesus used, when he said this, was the common sparrow. Sparrows are everywhere; they're very ordinary and, by our standards, not at all important. Yet Jesus said that God oversees even sparrow disasters! "Not one of them will fall to the ground apart from your Father," he said.

God is the absolute sovereign of the universe. He rules everything; nothing is independent of his control. If something could happen that was against God's will, that thing would be greater than God. Sometimes people like to think that God is only behind the good things that happen, the things that make people happy. They think that a good God could never cause the birth of a baby with birth defects or a violent earthquake that kills thousands or a war. Yet God clearly claims responsibility for all these things. If they happened apart from his will, whatever caused them would be greater than he is.

Jesus used this truth to encourage his people to have no fear of those who hated him (and them) and who would try to silence them by hurting or even killing them. It isn't that Christ's followers will never face disasters, suffering, or death. Rather, the only things that can touch them will be those things that God allows. If he allows them, they will turn out to produce good in the long run, and he will protect his people from any eternal harm.

As for me and my house . . .

- To see that God controls even the things that cause grief and pain, read the following verses: Exodus 4:11; Amos 3:6; Isaiah 45:7; Lamentations 3:37–38.

- Read Romans 8:28 to see how God will use such things in the lives of his people.

33

Under His Wings
A Reliable Refuge

"He who dwells in the shelter of the Most High
will abide in the shadow of the Almighty. . . .
He will cover you with his pinions,
and under his wings you will find refuge;
his faithfulness is a shield and buckler."

Psalm 91:1, 4

Have you ever visited a barnyard? Were there chickens? Did any of the hens have baby chicks? If so, when you walked toward them, they may have become frightened, not sure whether you were friend or foe. In that case, they would have scurried over to their mother, who would have lifted her wings enough for them to scurry under; then, she would have settled her wings back down over them to keep them safe.

The Bible uses this picture of baby birds finding protection under the wings of their mother as a metaphor for the safety God's people find in him. A refuge is a place free from what would harm. Hunters are not allowed in a wildlife refuge; birds and animals are safe there from being killed by humans. Our key verse describes finding refuge under God's wings. Whatever might harm or destroy cannot get to the one who hides there.

David used this word picture of baby birds protected by their mother's wings in several of his psalms. "Hide me in the shadow of your wings," he wrote, "from the wicked who do me violence, my deadly enemies who surround me" (Ps. 17:8–9). In another psalm, David prayed, "in the shadow of your wings I will take refuge, till the storms of destruction pass by" (Ps. 57:1).

What is God a refuge *from*? David asked for protection from the wicked, from deadly enemies surrounding him. He said he would take refuge under God's wings during "storms of destruction." God oversees what touches his people and allows only those things to hurt them that will be for their ultimate good, but he promises his people that they *will* have suffering. It isn't from everything we might find painful or uncomfortable that God promises to protect. Rather, God will keep his people from the enemy that would do violence to their souls and will protect them from the storms that would destroy. The enemies that would destroy souls are Satan and those he uses, and our own sin. These enemies would keep us from God if they could. The storm of destruction most to be feared is the promised storm of God's own wrath that will come, in his time, on all the earth.

God, in his grace, provides a refuge under his wings from his own wrath at sin. He provides protection from the damage our sin and Satan's hatred would do to us. But God's protection is only for those who take refuge in him. When Jesus was on earth, he looked out on the city of Jerusalem and its people who did not want him for a Savior, and lamented, "O Jerusalem, Jerusalem, the city that kills the prophets and stones those who are sent to it! How often would I have gathered your children together as a hen gathers her brood under her wings, and you would not!" (Matt. 23:37).

As for me and my house . . .

- Have you understood that your sin cuts you off from God's favor and makes you a target of God's wrath? Have you realized that God's great grace has provided a refuge from your sin and from God's wrath at it? Have you said, like David, "Be merciful to me, O God, be merciful to me, for in you my soul takes refuge . . ." (Ps. 57:1)?

Day 6

Animals and People

Look at All the Animals!
God's Wisdom on Display

"For every beast of the forest is mine,
the cattle on a thousand hills.
I know all the birds of the hills,
and all that moves in the field is mine."

Psalm 50:10–11

What would it have been like to have been the first human being and to have watched a parade of all the animals march past for you to name? Beautiful creatures, strange creatures, tiny insects, giant animals—all passing by in a display of animal diversity never to be duplicated. Adam would have been startled by the neck of one tall, odd-looking creature. Once he saw the giraffe nibbling at the leaves in high treetops, though, God's gift of a long neck for the giraffe would have made perfect sense to Adam.

Even more startling was the elephant's swinging trunk. How could such a nose be anything but in the way? But when Adam saw the many things the elephant could do with such a nose, he would have had nothing but admiration for this feature of God's creation. An elephant can suck up water with his nose and squirt it into his mouth. When you consider what a short neck the elephant has and how large and awkward his body is, you can see that it must be quite an advantage to have a nose that allows it to drink without having to bend down to a pond. The elephant can carry heavy loads with his trunk as well as pick up, with great precision, something tiny on the ground, like a twig. With his trunk, the elephant can pull the leaves from trees to put in his mouth or pick up the food he finds down at his feet. And since the elephant lives where it's hot, his trunk comes in handy for keeping cool. He can lift water over his head and squirt it on himself, as though he were taking a shower, and he can scoop up dust to cover his head and back, protecting himself from sunburn. But what about those ears? Who needs enormous, floppy ears like the elephant's? The elephant does, again because of his warm homeland. When he flaps his ears, not only do they act as giant fans to cool him, but the blood flowing through the many blood vessels in his ears becomes cooled as well, and as it travels on, it cools the rest of his body.

God designed all his creatures so their needs would be met and they would be able to live in his world. Consider how your cat can move about in almost absolute silence, making it good at sneaking up on any prey it wants to catch. Consider its ability to leap up walls and fences and jump down on the other side without hurting itself. Or think of your dog's super sense of smell. And then there are all those animals that God has made able to melt into their surroundings, to hide from enemies or from prey (such as the crocodile that lies patiently like a log in the water until lunch walks up or the chameleon that changes color). Think of the protective devices God has given some animals: quills to the porcupine and "fragranced" spray to the skunk.

How many and how wonderful are all God's designs for the creatures he made!

As for me and my house . . .

- Time for a trip to the zoo! Take the time to read the information posted about the animals, to learn more of how wisely God made each animal you see. Be prepared to read that the unique features of these animals just evolved over time. Sin darkens hearts so completely that people are unable to see the design and wisdom of God that appears so obviously in the animals he has made.

35

Who Cares for Wild Beasts?

God's Provision for His Creatures

"The eyes of all look to you,
and you give them their food in due season.
You open your hand;
you satisfy the desire of every living thing."

Psalm 145:15–16

It's a dog's life" used to mean "it's an unpleasant kind of life." That was back when most dogs lived outside, no matter what the weather. Now, however, "a dog's life" could be another way to say "the good life!" Now, dogs live in the house, some in their own furnished bedrooms. Dogs wear booties and sweaters for added comfort. Instead of dog sitters, there are doggy hotels, even resorts. There are bakeries that make only baked treats for dogs. People take dogs to doggy "happy hour," where they "mingle" and eat treats with their doggy friends. There are even ways now to include your dog in your wedding!

What about the wild animals, though? Who looks out for them? All over the world, in every kind of environment on our planet, animals eat, sleep in their homes, and have and raise babies with no help at all from any of us. We all know this and take it for granted. Of course, the wild animals don't need humans; they're usually better off without us. Nonetheless, many things the animals do and need are quite complicated.

Remember our poem back in chapter 2 that said, "Earth's crammed with heaven, and every common bush afire with God"? Everywhere on earth, God actively cares for his creation. "And only he who sees takes off his shoes." If we look at nature with all its creatures through eyes trained by Scripture, we understand that the complex relationships creatures have with each other and with their habitats were designed that way by God. We see that when animals do incredible things, it's by instincts that God gave them. When animals have enough to eat and drink, it's because God provides it. Those who don't look at nature through the eyes of Scripture don't "see"; they "sit around it [the bush afire with God] and pluck blackberries." They enjoy what they can of nature while completely missing the wonders of God's wisdom and faithfulness that these things reveal. Instead, they say, things are as they are because, just by chance, over millions of years, they happened to evolve this way.

Those who see realize that the young lions seek their prey from God (Ps. 104:21). They know that God provides the prey for the ravens when their young cry for food (Job 38:41). Those who see realize that it isn't by chance that rain falls on the mountains, creating streams where wild animals quench their thirst and by whose waters tall trees grow, providing homes for the birds. God causes these things to happen (Ps. 104:10–13).

Those who look through eyes trained by Scripture realize that God causes the grass to grow for the livestock as well as the plants on humans' farms (Ps. 104:14). Those who see know that God is watching over the births of the wild goats, off in their isolated habitats, bringing the baby animals to be born at just the right point in their development, providing what the mothers need as they give birth (Job 39:1–4).

Those who see realize that it is by God's hand that every living creature breathes and lives. Were he to withdraw his hand, all would instantly perish (Ps. 104:27–29). Those who see notice God's faithful provision all through nature and worship him for it. They "take off their shoes," because wherever they look, God is there.

As for me and my house . . .

- Look up all the verses cited in this reading and read them from God's Word. Let them lead you to praise God for his wonderful care for his creatures.

36

God Owns the Animals

Daniel and the Lions

Daniel 6

"The LORD has established his throne in the heavens,
and his kingdom rules over all."

Psalm 103:19

T he last sliver of glowing sun sank below the horizon. Darius was out of time. He had spent the day trying to escape the trap they had set for him, but the trap still held. There was no way out. It didn't matter that he'd been tricked and lured into this trap by deceit. It didn't matter that Daniel, the one whom the trap would destroy, was the next-in-charge after the king, and the one Darius could best trust. Nor did it matter that King Darius ruled the greatest empire of the day. None of that could spring the trap and save Daniel's life.

Darius heard the approaching footsteps of those who had set this nasty trap, the very men he himself had set in positions of power to serve him and the empire. He sighed. They entered, insisting that he enforce the law they'd asked him to sign, reminding him that a law of the Medes and Persians forbade the changing of any law the king had established.

And he had established the law. These men had come to him earlier, asking that he sign into law an order forbidding people to pray to anyone other than himself, the king, for thirty days. Darius had thought they were just trying to establish his authority and to call for a show of loyalty from his subjects. It would be good for the kingdom. How wise of them to have thought of it! But then these men had returned to tell him that Daniel had broken the new law. Daniel had opened his windows, which he did three times every day, and had prayed to his God in plain view. That's when Darius knew that he'd been tricked. Those men had no interest in what was best for the kingdom. They just wanted to get rid of Daniel because they were jealous of him.

The king had no choice but to cast Daniel into a den of lions, the punishment required for breaking this law. But as he did, he said to Daniel, "May your God, whom you serve continually, deliver you!" And he sealed the stone blocking the den's entrance with his own ring.

Darius went back to his palace and paced back and forth, back and forth. He wouldn't eat and he wouldn't sleep. He spent the night waiting for dawn, when he could reopen the den. At the very first light of day, the king hurried back to the lions' den, ordering it to be opened and crying out, "Daniel! Was your God able to keep you from the lions?"

Darius almost melted with relief when he heard the strong voice of Daniel call back, "My God sent his angel and shut the lions' mouths, and they have not harmed me!" Darius called for Daniel to be lifted out of the den and had the men who had wanted Daniel destroyed, along with their families, thrown in with the lions. With no angel to hold them back, the lions overpowered Daniel's enemies before they even reached the bottom of the den, breaking all their bones in pieces.

At this, Darius understood that Daniel's God lives, rules, and is to be feared. He can do what even the greatest ruler on earth cannot, and even fierce lions will obey him. The kingdom of Daniel's God will never end.

As for me and my house . . .

• For additional stories of animals obeying God's command, read Numbers 22:22–35; 1 Kings 13:11–28; and Jonah 1:17; 2:10; 4:6–11.

37

Behold, the Lion of the Tribe of Judah!

Victorious Lord

"Judah is a lion's cub. . . .
The scepter shall not depart from Judah,
nor the ruler's staff from between his feet,
until tribute comes to him;
and to him shall be the obedience of the peoples."

Genesis 49:9–10

"Behold, the Lion of the tribe of Judah, the Root of David, has conquered. . . ."

Revelation 5:5

What descriptive words come to mind when you hear the word "lion"? Powerful? Kingly? Fierce? Scripture speaks of the Lord Jesus Christ as a lion. Centuries before Jesus was born, Jacob, father of the twelve tribes of Israel, spoke the words of the prophecy in our key verse (Gen. 49:9–10). He compared his son Judah and his descendants to a lion. Since he's a lion, Jacob said, "who dares rouse him?" Then he went on to add that someone from Judah would always rule, and the peoples of earth would obey him.

The promise was partially fulfilled when David, of the tribe of Judah, became king of God's people. When Jesus was born, the promise had its fuller fulfillment, since Jesus was from the tribe of Judah and would rule all people.

How is Jesus like a lion? He is powerful; he is kingly; and he is fierce. In the Old Testament, God spoke of how he would judge his disobedient people. "I am to them like a lion; like a leopard I will lurk beside the way. I will fall upon them like a bear robbed of her cubs; I will tear open their breast, and there I will devour them like a lion, as a wild beast would rip them open" (Hos. 13:7–8).

The New Testament book of Revelation describes Jesus returning in judgment. The writer sees him coming on a white horse, and says, "From his mouth comes a sharp sword with which to strike down the nations, and he will rule them with a rod of iron. He will tread the winepress of the fury of the wrath of God the Almighty" (Rev. 19:15).

If you came upon a lion in the wild, you would treat him with respect! You would be very careful not to tease him or make him angry. He could run upon you quickly, hold you down with his powerful paw, and tear you apart. As grim as an attack by an angry lion would be, it would be infinitely worse to have the Son of God come against you in anger. This is why it is so important to respond to his offer of grace for sinners now, while you can. He has all power, and his anger at sin is fierce.

We call the lion the "king of the beasts." Jesus is the king over all. The psalmist wrote of God the Father saying to God the Son, "Ask of me, and I will make the nations your heritage, and the ends of the earth your possession. You shall break them with a rod of iron and dash them in pieces like a potter's vessel" (Ps. 2:8–9).

If a lion gets in a fight with some other creature, chances are the lion will come out on top! Lions win. In the book of Revelation, John saw a scroll in the hand of God, sealed up with seals so that it couldn't be opened. A search was made in heaven and earth for someone worthy to open those seals, but none was found. John wept over this until he heard someone say, "Weep no more; behold, the Lion of the tribe of Judah, the Root of David, has conquered, so that he can open the scroll and its seven seals" (Rev. 5:5). The Lord Jesus Christ, the Lion of the tribe of Judah is powerful, fierce, kingly, and victorious.

As for me and my house . . .

- Read Acts 10:42–43 and 17:30–31 where the apostles call people to faith and repentance now because God will send his Son in judgment later. Make sure you've accepted God's offer of grace.

38

Behold, the Lamb of God!

Merciful Savior

"Behold, the Lamb of God, who takes away the sin of the world!"
John 1:29

John stopped crying. The voice had said, "Stop weeping. The Lion of the tribe of Judah has conquered, so he can open the seals." What a relief! In John's vision in Revelation, he had been standing in heaven during a great search for someone worthy to open the scroll in God's hand. Seven seals held the scroll shut; if the scroll were not opened, how could God's purposes be carried out? The search had been throughout the earth, under the earth, and even in heaven, and no one was found who was worthy to open the scroll. That was why John had been crying. Now the voice had said the Lion had conquered, and he could open the scrolls. John turned to see this conquering lion and saw instead a lamb. And this was not just any lamb, but a lamb standing as if slain.

Jesus is the lion. And Jesus is the lamb. He conquered by being killed.

How is Jesus like a lamb? For hundreds of years, God's people had killed lambs and had offered them as sacrifices for sin, as God had commanded. The people would place their hands on the lamb's head as it was being killed as a way of saying that their sin was placed on the animal and that its death was what they deserved. When John the Baptist saw Jesus coming toward him at the beginning of his ministry, John said, "Behold, the Lamb of God, who takes away the sin of the world!" All those slain lambs had been a picture of this Lamb. Jesus would take the sins of God's people on himself and then die in their place.

A lamb is just an animal, and its death cannot remove a single sin. Jesus is the Son of God, and his death is worth enough to pay for and remove every single sin of every one of his people.

A lamb is a gentle animal. When it's carried away to slaughter, it doesn't protest. Jesus willingly came to die for God's people. Although he hated the thought of bearing sin and of facing God's wrath, he wanted what God wanted. He didn't resist his enemies when they came for him, even though he knew they would crucify him. "He was oppressed, and he was afflicted, yet he opened not his mouth; like a lamb that is led to the slaughter, and like a sheep that before its shearers is silent, so he opened not his mouth" (Isa. 53:7).

If a lamb gets into a fight with another creature, the lamb will probably lose. It has no way of hurting anything and no way of resisting. Jesus was a lamb. He didn't resist his enemies but allowed them to do whatever they wished with him. He didn't fight back, and so he lost and they won. They had their way and killed him. But it was in his defeat that he conquered. In his death, Jesus accomplished God's purpose of redeeming a people for himself. The enemies of God had worked hard to prevent this, but Jesus defeated them all by dying.

Jesus calls his followers to follow his pattern of victory through suffering. We must not expect to have everything easy in this life, but must be prepared to suffer, confident that in the end the victory belongs to the Lamb.

As for me and my house . . .

- Give thanks to our Savior for dying in the place of his people and for conquering through defeat.
- See what Jesus calls his followers to in Matthew 5:11–12; Luke 9:23–24; John 15:18–20; and Revelation 12:10–11.

In the Image of God
God's Grace in Man's Creation

"So God created man in his own image,
in the image of God he created him;
male and female he created them."

Genesis 1:27

Has it ever occurred to you that you could have begun life as a snail? Or a bunny rabbit or a sparrow? Think of how different your life would be, and think of how different you would be! There are hundreds of thousands of different kinds of creatures in our world, and all are wonderful and demonstrate the creative wisdom of God. None of those creatures, though, can begin to compare with the human being. To humans alone God gave his best and most gracious gifts. Of humans alone, God said, "Let us make man in our image, after our likeness . . ." (Gen. 1:26).

Part of being made in God's image is having the ability to learn about and use so many other parts of God's creation. A field mouse will eat the grains it needs, drink water, burrow into the dirt, and line its nest with odds and ends it finds. It has no interest in the rest of God's creation. Humans, however, use almost everything God has made, and they're still discovering new uses for things.

A bird can build a nest for itself that is exactly the kind of nest it needs. But it doesn't decorate the nest. It doesn't consider several different kinds of architecture and then choose its favorite. It never builds huge skyscraper nests that many little bird families could live in. Only to humans did God give the ability to create, like he does. Of course, God creates out of nothing, while humans need materials. Still, a human is unlike any other creature, because a human can have an idea for a painting or a quilt or a statue or a computer game, a new idea no one else has ever had, and can gather what he or she needs to make something from that idea.

Many animals, birds, and fish migrate every year. They travel great distances at one season, then when the seasons change, they travel back again. They do this completely by instinct as an amazing part of God's design. Humans, however, can think and plan, remember and imagine. They can plan what they'll do next week, along with each step needed to do it. They can imagine things they've never experienced. They can think through issues and make decisions. This is unique among God's creatures. The ability to think and reason is God's gift to us.

Horses can call to each other or let each other know when they're angry. But they can't tell each other what they're thinking or what they did last Sunday. Humans, like God, are able to communicate a wealth of information, feelings, and ideas. They can even record their communications in writing so people living hundreds of years later can know what they thought.

And what about right and wrong? If a bear kills another bear in a fight, is it guilty? No, it's just an animal. It doesn't know any better. God gave humans the knowledge of right and wrong. They're moral creatures. They have a conscience.

Best of all, humans can know God. Dogs like the people who care for them. They wag their tails when they see them and lick their hands. But you can't teach a dog about God. A dog can't worship. It can't pray. God made humans in his image so they could know him, love him, enjoy him, and worship him. He made us so we can have a relationship with him that will last forever. What a gracious gift!

As for me and my house . . .

- God created humans with these special abilities so they could know him and give him glory. Go back through this reading and consider how you could use each of the specifically "human" things listed for the purposes of enjoying God and glorifying him.

Fearfully and Wonderfully Made

God's Wisdom Seen in Our Bodies

"For just as the body is one and has many members, and all the members of the body, though many, are one body, so it is with Christ."

1 Corinthians 12:12

Think back to the last time you hurt yourself so that you began to bleed. Why did the bleeding stop? You need your blood, of course, to carry food and oxygen to the trillions of cells in your body. If you lost all your blood, or even a great deal of it, your body couldn't continue to live. That makes life in this world a dangerous business, doesn't it? After all, your skin's not all that tough. Sometimes you can make a cut in it with just a piece of paper!

One of the wise and amazing things about the way God designed you is this: he created platelets in your blood so that you wouldn't bleed to death every time you got scraped. When platelets, flowing through your body in your blood, come to an injury, they gather right there, sticking to each other like glue and forming a blood clot. The clot plugs up the cut so blood can't come out. Eventually, the clot will harden into a scab and will remain over the injury until new skin grows underneath.

Stand up and look down at your feet. They aren't very big in comparison with the rest of your body. Yet you can stand erect on those feet without worrying about toppling over like a tall tower of blocks built on two small ones. God made you with a hard skeleton that holds you erect. In those two little feet with their ankles he put fifty-two bones that all work together to keep you standing straight. If they didn't work correctly, you would find it impossible to keep your balance. Wave your hand and wiggle your fingers. You can do that because God arranged fifty-four bones in your wrists, hands, and fingers just right, so they would work together.

And we could go on—with your digestive system, your nervous system that sends messages from the brain to the rest of your body and back again, your muscles, and on and on. God arranged it all wisely and well.

In several places in the New Testament, the apostle Paul compared the church to a human body. Like a body with its many different parts all doing different tasks but working together for the good of the whole body, the people of God have many different members. All the members have their own spiritual gifts and their own areas of ministry; they're not all the same. Imagine, Paul wrote, a body in which every part's job was seeing, or in which every part's job was hearing. How would the body walk or talk or get work done?

And just as all the members of a body take care of each other, so all the members of Christ's body should take care of each other. When one toe is sore, your whole body rearranges things to try to keep that toe from hurting. When one member or one part of the church suffers or struggles, the rest of God's people should do all they can to help.

When God's people work together, caring for each other and carrying out their own tasks, the whole church grows and is healthy, for the glory of God.

As for me and my house . . .

- Read Psalm 139:13–16, where David marvels at how God formed him while he was still in his mother and no one could see him. Praise God because you, too, are "fearfully and wonderfully made."

- Read the passages in which Paul shows how the church is like a human body: Romans 12:4–8; 1 Corinthians 12:12–27; and Ephesians 4:4–16. Are you doing your part in the body and are you caring for other members?

41

Body and Soul

The Creation of Adam and the Coming of Christ

*"Then the L*ORD *God formed the man of dust from the ground and breathed into his nostrils the breath of life, and the man became a living creature."*
Genesis 2:7

"And the Word became flesh and dwelt among us. . . ."
John 1:14

One way that humans are different from angels is this: God created humans as spirit and body. Angels are spirit only. Out of the dust of the earth, God created Adam's body. God made Adam's muscles and nerves, heart and brain. God gave Adam bones and blood and hands and feet and covered him all over with skin. Adam *looked* perfect, but he could do nothing; he wasn't alive. Then God breathed into his nostrils, and Adam became a living soul. Many years later, when Adam died, it was because his soul (or spirit) had left his body.

God created us, on purpose, as soul *and* body. The soul is the "inside" part of us, the part that thinks and worships and makes choices. The soul is where our personality is, the part of us that makes us different from anyone else. Our bodies are our "outsides"; they enable us to enjoy God's wonderful creation. We can see the beauty he made and hear the many sounds he built into his world. Our bodies feel warm sun, cool breezes, and loving hugs. Our noses smell flowers and baking brownies, while our tongues can savor the thousands of different flavors God created for our food.

Our bodies are a gift, but not everyone has always understood that. Somewhere back in history, the idea developed that the human spirit is important and the human body is not. Some have even said the human body is evil. This isn't the Bible's view. God "richly provides us with everything to enjoy" (1 Tim. 6:17); he also graciously provides bodies with which to enjoy everything.

When Jesus came to save us, he became a human being, fully and completely. Jesus took a real human body that would be able to enjoy all God's gifts but would also experience hunger, exhaustion, pain, and death. Jesus also took a real human spirit. Human beings had failed to obey their Creator and had given in to temptation instead. To save them, Jesus had to resist temptation and obey God perfectly *as a human being*. God's people had earned death for their rebellion against him. To save them, Jesus had to die in their place, which he could only do if he were a human being.

When Jesus rose from the dead, it was his real human body that rose. His spirit came back into his body, and his disciples saw him as a real, flesh-and-blood man. They saw and touched the wounds in his body from his crucifixion. He even ate fish with them, to make sure they understood he had a real body. When Jesus went back into heaven, he took his human body and spirit with him. When he returns to judge all men and to take his people to be with him in heaven, people will see him, because he will return in his visible human body.

Jesus will keep his human body and spirit forever. He will continue forever to be the only being in the universe to be completely, truly God and completely, truly human. We never need to think of our bodies as evil or un-important, because God the Son has and will always keep a body like ours.

As for me and my house . . .

- Thank God for all the things you can do with your amazing body.
- Thank God for giving you a soul that makes you wonderfully different from the animals.
- Praise Jesus for becoming just like us (except for sin) in order to save us.

Reason for Being
Created for God's Glory

"So, whether you eat or drink, or whatever you do,
do all to the glory of God."
1 Corinthians 10:31

A creature is a creature. A creature is not God. People often make the mistake of acting as if they were God. King Nebuchadnezzar took all the credit for the mighty empire he ruled. Though God had revealed to him in several attention-grabbing ways that it is God who raises up rulers and takes them down again, Nebuchadnezzar still prided himself on ruling his great empire. One day, as the king looked from the palace roof and saw the glittering city of Babylon at his feet, he just couldn't help saying, "Is not this great Babylon, which I have built by my mighty power . . . for the glory of my majesty?" (Dan. 4:30). At that very moment, God took away Nebuchadnezzar's sanity. Not only was the king *not* God, now he would not even act like a man. Nebuchadnezzar believed he was a wild animal and went to live out in the fields, his hair and nails growing long like an animal's. This would last, a voice from heaven told Nebuchadnezzar, "until you know that the Most High rules the kingdom of men and gives it to whom he will" (Dan. 4:32). Nebuchadnezzar eventually recovered and was very careful to "praise and extol and honor the King of heaven," because, Nebuchadnezzar said, "those who walk in pride he is able to humble" (Dan. 4:37).

King Herod (Agrippa I) is another example of a man who thought he was as powerful as God. After trying to stop God's gospel from spreading by beheading the apostle James and planning to execute the apostle Peter, Herod began to notice his limitations. First, the night before Peter was scheduled to die, God sent an angel who opened Peter's locked door, removed his chains, and led him out of the secure and well-guarded prison. When the soldiers came to execute Peter, he was nowhere to be found. Herod learned nothing from this, and he went off to give a speech to some of his subjects. He was delighted when they began to cheer and applaud for him, calling out that his was the voice of a god and not a man. Herod gladly received such praise, and God struck him dead with a gruesome disease that involved worms eating him. Herod didn't seem so godlike then!

These two kings aren't the only creatures who wanted to believe they were God. At the very beginning of human history, Satan told Eve it was safe to ignore God's command to not eat the fruit of the tree of the knowledge of good and evil. Not only would it not hurt her, Satan assured Eve, the fruit would also *make her like God*. Eve decided that was what she wanted. It wasn't enough to be a creature, not even a creature made in God's image and with many gifts and privileges. Eve wanted to be just like God.

Ever since, all of us have wanted to be God. We want what we want, when we want it. We have a hard time believing that we really aren't the center of the universe. We need to remind ourselves all the time that God is God and we are not. God created all that is, including us, for his glory. Our whole reason for existing is to give him glory, not to have our way or to get glory for ourselves.

As for me and my house . . .

- If you've never memorized the first answer in the Westminster Shorter Catechism, this would be a good time to do it:

  Q. What is the chief end of man?
  A. The chief end of man is to glorify God and to enjoy him forever.

- Our key verse is also good to memorize. It's easy to learn, but living by its rule can be challenging!

Obeying the Creator
Adam's Failure and Christ's Success

*"For as by the one man's disobedience the many were made sinners, so by
the one man's obedience the many will be made righteous."*
Romans 5:19

What creature does *not* obey its Creator? Light-filled day follows light-filled day, until God calls for three days of constant darkness in Egypt. Then three dark days result. Light-weight things float and heavy things sink until God calls for an axe head to float to the surface of a river, and it obeys. Century after century, people walk on the earth with no fear of holes opening and swallowing them, until God commands the earth to open and swallow a group of rebels. Only living plants produce first buds, then blossoms, and finally fruit, but when God commands a dead stick—a man's staff—to bud, blossom, and bear fruit all in one night, it obeys. Sun, moon, and stars follow their God-ordained paths, until God himself interrupts them. When God gives the command, scavenger birds carry food to a human, fish gather in one place to be caught, and lions refuse to attack. Only one creature on the planet fails to obey God, and that is man.

Of all creatures, humans have the most reason to obey God. They have been made in his image and given valuable abilities the other creatures lack. They can know, enjoy, and love God. They have been given the entire earth for meeting their needs. God also gave humans the ability to make choices, and, sad to say, they chose foolishly. Beginning with Adam and Eve in the garden of Eden, humans have consistently chosen to do things their way, not God's. They have consistently chosen created things before the Creator. They have consistently chosen disobedience. In fact, because of Adam's first wrong choice, humans are no longer even capable of obeying God. They are sinners, and sin comes as natural to them as flight does to a bird.

Back in Eden, Adam represented all mankind. When he sinned, he sinned on behalf of all of us, so sin spread to us all. God in his grace, however, provided a second chance for mankind, a way to bring his people back to obedience. God gave his son, Jesus, to represent all God's people. Jesus never gave in to the least temptation. He lived his whole life in perfect obedience to the Father, and he did this in the place of his people. Those who put their faith in Jesus can present to God Jesus' perfect obedience instead of their sin; God counts every righteous act of his Son as though such people had done it themselves.

And that isn't all! God not only counts the obedience of Jesus as belonging to the one who believes in him, God also works in that person to cause him or her to grow in being obedient. When people put their faith in Christ, the Holy Spirit comes to live in them and to work in them and change them so their greatest desire is to live for God. The Holy Spirit works in God's people as long as they live, making them able to obey God and to grow steadily more like Christ.

As for me and my house . . .

In Peter's first sermon, he told his hearers what God commands all people in all places to do, as well as what they would receive if they did it. "Repent and be baptized every one of you in the name of Jesus Christ for the forgiveness of your sins, and you will receive the gift of the Holy Spirit. For the promise is for you and for your children and for all who are far off, everyone whom the Lord our God calls to himself" (Acts 2:38–39). Have you obeyed this most important commandment and received this most valuable gift?

Saved, Body and Soul
God's Promise of a Resurrection

"For the Lord himself will descend from heaven with a cry of command, with the voice of an archangel, and with the sound of the trumpet of God. And the dead in Christ will rise first. Then we who are alive, who are left, will be caught up together with them in the clouds to meet the Lord in the air, and so we will always be with the Lord."

1 Thessalonians 4:16–17

It had been bad enough when the first one had died. All the encouragement the new Christians in Thessalonica had received from this dear Christian friend when they had suffered persecution together, all the hopes they had shared with him of the joy they would know when Jesus returned from heaven for them—all that was ended. He had died, just like nonbelievers did. He would never encourage them again, but even worse, he wouldn't be here when Jesus returned for them! Then another member of the church grew sick and died. Another one would miss Jesus' return. Why hadn't Jesus come back *before* these dear people had died?

So, of course, when Timothy came from Paul, checking up on how the Thessalonian Christians were doing, they let him know right away of their tremendous disappointment, even their despair, over their dead friends who would miss Jesus' return for the church.

As soon as Paul heard this report from Timothy, he sent a letter to the Thessalonians. He hurried to reassure them that their friends were not dead forever. When Jesus returned for his people, even before he took those still living to be with him, he would raise his people who had died. This is why, Paul wrote, when believers die, their friends don't need to grieve in despair like nonbelievers who have no hope. Believers know they will be reunited with their believing loved ones.

Paul wrote to the Christians in Corinth about this same matter in much more detail. People there were denying that there would be a resurrection. Paul wanted them to know that just as Jesus' body rose from the grave, so believers' bodies will be raised from the grave as well. As for those who are alive when Jesus returns, their bodies will be changed. Now, because of sin, our bodies are perishable; they die. Our new bodies will be imperishable. When a dead body is buried, that body is either marred because of an injury of some kind or it has weakened and possibly grown ugly through disease or old age. Our new bodies will be beautiful, glorious, and strong forever. The Bible says of the dead body of a Christian: "It is sown in dishonor; it is raised in glory. It is sown in weakness; it is raised in power" (1 Cor. 15:43). And this transformation will take place instantly when Jesus returns, "in a moment, in the twinkling of an eye" (1 Cor. 15:52). At our Lord's powerful word, every ash and every particle of each dead body, no matter how long it's been dead, will come together in a moment to form a new, glorious body that will live forever with Christ.

What a powerful Lord we have! What hope and joy we can have for the future, even when we grow old or sick or when we watch Christians we love die. Our Lord, who created us body and soul, who redeemed us and cared for us all through life, will also bring us, body and soul, to be with him forever. We will love and enjoy him then even better than we now do.

As for me and my house . . .

- Read the whole passage in 1 Corinthians 15:12–58 about the resurrection of believers and read Paul's encouragement to the Thessalonians in 1 Thessalonians 4:13–18.

Lord of Creation
A New Heavens and Earth

*"And he who was seated on the throne said, 'Behold,
I am making all things new.' . . ."*
Revelation 21:5

At the end of each creation day, God looked at what he had made and "saw that it was good." At the end of the creation week, he looked at everything and saw that it was "very good." All God made calls us to worship him for his wisdom, his power, his goodness, and his sovereignty. For those whose eyes have been opened to see, "every common bush" causes them to "take off their shoes" in worship.

At the same time, though, everywhere we look we also see what is sad, evil, and ugly. The perfect creation God made has been marred by the sin of the one earthly creature who refused to obey, man. From baby birds falling from their nests to tsunami waves that take the lives of thousands, all creation shows the effects of sin. Man, the disobedient creature, causes untold suffering to his fellow men and to the rest of creation. From toddlers who pinch their baby brothers to serial killers who murder many people, human beings hurt each other. From polluting the air to deliberately torturing animals, humans hurt their world.

God is the Lord of his creation, though. He did not create his universe to be this way, and he will not leave it like this. As soon as sin entered the world, God promised to repair what sin had broken. He promised a child who would crush the head of the serpent who tempted man to sin. Of course, that child turned out to be the Lord Jesus Christ. He died for the sins of his people on the cross. He changes their hearts and gives them the

Holy Spirit, making them able to obey and to become holy. He promises to take them to heaven where they will be perfect in holiness.

But that's not all! God has also promised that, in Christ, he will free the whole creation from the effects of sin (Rom. 8:19–22). God has "a plan for the fullness of time, to unite all things in him [Christ], things in heaven and things on earth" (Eph. 1:10). The prophets promise a new heaven and earth, a place from which all that hurts and harms will be absent and there will be no death, no mourning, no crying, no pain, no tears, and no sin of any kind.

In the new heaven and earth, God will be everything. "For the earth will be filled with the knowledge of the glory of the Lord as the waters cover the sea" (Hab. 2:14). Those who are there will love, worship, serve, and enjoy him perfectly. As for those who never gave him the glory he deserved, they will realize their mistake, but it will be too late.

Creation had a beginning. It has a goal, and God, its originator, moves it steadily along toward that goal. While sin has filled creation with horrors of all kinds, much of the beauty and glory God built into it remain to show him to those who see. Those who see serve him as their Lord now while they wait in hope for him to make all things new.

As for me and my house . . .

- Peter tells us that the Lord delays his coming to give people time to come to him in repentance. If you have not yet turned to Christ in faith, you have nothing to expect from his return but judgment. Don't wait until it's too late, but confess Jesus Christ as Lord and Savior now.

- Peter also asks you who do know Christ as Savior, who do hope for this new heaven and earth, to consider "what sort of people ought you to be in lives of holiness and godliness" (2 Pet. 3:11) while you wait.

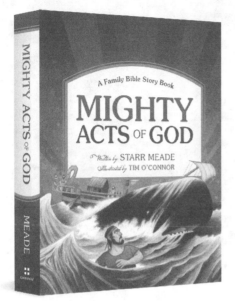

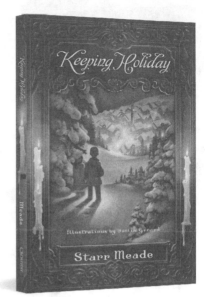

Mighty Acts of God

Designed for families with children ages 4–10, this Bible story book teaches about God's character by taking a panoramic, chronological look at his mighty acts of redemption. Ninety Bible stories are retold in modern language and followed by discussion-sparking application questions for the whole family.

HC, 978-1-4335-0604-8, $24.99

Keeping Holiday

From the heart of a teacher and grandparent comes this vividly illustrated book that families can read together to experience the wonder of the Incarnation and come to know the "Founder of Holiday." Young Dylan's adventures also provide a charming way for children to discover how God brings a person to faith. *Suited for children ages 5 and up.*

TPB, 978-1-4335-0142-5, $14.99

God's Mighty Acts in Salvation

Forty interactive readings for children ages 8–12 unpack Paul's teachings in Galatians about God's saving work and the gospel. Great for children to read alone or with parents or teachers.

TPB, 978-1-4335-1401-2, $10.99

The Most Important Thing You'll Ever Study

This overview of the Bible uses an easy-to-follow study guide format to teach students ages 12–16 the central messages and narratives of Scripture, helping them grow in knowledge and love for God's Word.

FULL SET: 978-1-4335-1182-0, $54.99

Volumes 1, 2, & 5 (Old Testament with Answer Key): 978-1-4335-2028-0, $32.99
Volumes 3, 4, & 5 (New Testament with Answer Key): 978-1-4335-2045-7, $32.99
Volumes 1 & 2 (Old Testament): 978-1-4335-2024-2, $27.99
Volumes 3 & 4 (New Testament): 978-1-4335-2032-7, $27.99